# WHEN DARKNESS TURNS TO LIGHT

**ROY MACKPENFIELD**

MORGAN PUBLISHING
CARDIFF

Published in Wales by Morgan Publishing

post@morgan-publishing.co.uk
www.morgan-publishing.co.uk

ISBN: 1 903532 086

British Library Cataloguing-in-Publication Data.
A catalogue record for this book is available from the British Library.

# ACKNOWLEDGEMENTS

I would like to thank the following people for their contributions to the creation of this work.

Kay — The tutor who gave me the inspiration to explore talents I never knew existed.

Goff and Phil — Two of the best. For their invaluable contribution of IT knowledge and tuition in putting the pieces together.

Rhos — For her unselfish attitude and encouragement at times when my affliction hinders my progress. Rhos is always there to calm my fears.

Lynda — A great friend. She read the endless jumble of words, which I was unable to do.

My editor, Cath — For her unfailing faith in my ability and the encouragement she gave me to achieve my goal. Without her support this project may never have got off the ground

And last but not least,

Mr Cooling — The man without whom none of this would have been possible. By saving what was left of my sight he gave me a reason to dream of what else might be possible.

*This story is*
*Dedicated to my*
*Children and Grandchildren.*

*The gift of sight is arguably our most precious sense. To suffer lost sight is something that most cannot contemplate. Those who pass though such a nightmare and emerge surely deserve our at most admiration.*

Mr R J Cooling FRCS FRC Ophth.

.

# CONTENTS

# INTRODUCTION

From a catalogue of tragedies in childhood, the unquestioned respect and obedience of traditional Christian values penetrated his soul during those nurturing years and taught him tolerance.

With a disability at the age of two and constant taunts and pain, it is difficult to comprehend the will it took. However, with the author's Christian upbringing and the love and protection of his family, he learnt to take advantage of opportunities as they arose.

Against all odds, this young disabled Jamaican excelled in school, became a successful engineer in the hostile racial atmosphere of the sixties and seventies and has fulfilled many of his early dreams. This courage and inner strength gave him the desire and determination to put pen to paper and tell his remarkable story.

The lesson of this story must be to pursue our dreams with determination and respect, but never to forget our roots. Disability is not an excuse for failure, but can be means of exploring our talents and strengths in our own unique way.

# WHEN DARKNESS TURNS TO LIGHT

The infectious laughter of playful children echoes through the trees, streaming mid-summer sunrays light up the partly ripened leaves, with bees and butterflies feeding in beds of roses. The graceful stream with crystal waters sparkles over sun kissed rocks. The children scream with delight as they run in a circle. Their hands fill with freshly cut grass, blown across the path to create a glistering display. It brings excitement to neighbours, who lovingly tend to their plants. I feel humble and privileged to experience such a perfect moment in one of the most beautiful parts of Wales – a country where humanity and nature live in perfect harmony. The day could not have gone any better, the image no more perfect, no company more warming. The visit could not have been more rewarding.

I take for granted my childhood days in Jamaica, wrapped in the protective arms of my family. A country where the climate allows many varieties of fruit trees to flourish. With free and fearless hearts, my brother and I climbed the trees to stretch ourselves along the delicate branches selecting the biggest and ripest of the fruit. I take for granted my youthful days; the freedom to explore and make friends, a brilliant mind and the zest to learn life's meaning. I play the dangerous game of 'buggy ride'. The 'buggy' was made from a plank of wood, the axle from a section of the branch secured to the plank by twigs or twines. The round, smooth surfaces of the breadfruit plant make it ideal for the wheels. Grated husks of the cocoa beans are used as axle-grease. Dragged to the top of a mountainside our feet act as brakes. We would set off freewheeling down the uneven surface, bumping through the grass and shrubs in the hope that we would reach the bottom in one piece.

I take for granted my young adult days, when I was energetic with an appetite to learn all that lay beyond tomorrow's dreams. I take for granted the opportunity to travel from Jamaica to England to finish my engineering training, to enjoy the pleasure of girls, of drinking and dancing. I could achieve more than I ever had dreamed of, I could be promoted at work, I could marry and have five wonderful children in a home full of joy. I was the owner of two businesses, new cars every two years, four holidays per year. I could provide the family with the best available and give the children a good outlook with which to grow up.

I take for granted that at the tender age of two years I lost one eye, a disability I will not accept. I have done most things, except drive a coach, or a train, nor have I piloted a plane.

I take for granted that I am getting old, and less tolerant to stressful conditions like diabetes, high blood-pressure and arthritis that disrupt my life. I could become blind at any moment by overworking the remaining eye, removing the source of learning that is vital to my survival. The possibility of blindness and its implications never entered my head. But, I have no regrets. The experiences have given me strength.

The unfortunate event that is about to be revealed has spanned over four years. I had reached the plateau of my achievement. Matured at fifty-five, with a successful catering business. The children have grown up. They have taken on responsibility and left me to enjoy the comfort of holidays and pension plans. There was no thought given to what took place.

# Chapter 1

# TRAGEDY

Summer had reached its peek on a dry day with a light cool breeze. One Sunday at three o'clock in the afternoon, the fourth day of August 1998 a tragedy unfolded. My daughter and granddaughter joined my wife, stepdaughter and me for Sunday dinner. We ate together, we talked about our daily routines and our future plans. We catch up with the latest news. The children were restless wanting to do what they like best, to play. We watched the baby running around with other children sharing her excitement.

It seemed a shame to waste the beautiful weather sitting at home.

My daughters suggested a stroll to the park to enjoy the beauty we always took for granted. I had been working since the early hours that day and was feeling rather tired. I declined the invitation to walk, opting for a well-deserved rest. Whether that was the right decision, I will never know. One thing I know the sudden peace and quiet that filled the house was wonderfully relaxing. In that relaxed frame of mind, a smoke from my peace pipe was just what I needed. I picked up the pipe, giving it a good clean, but halfway into the cleaning I was overcome by an experience that shocked and frightened me.

A funny sensation began to creep across my vision, as if some kind of liquid was flowing inside my eye and was rapidly spreading in the path of my sight. At first my brain could not absorb what was happening. It appears I was seeing through someone else's eye. I quickly removed my glasses hastily cleaning and replacing them, but nothing changed. I ran to the bathroom, I washed my face realising the seriousness of the situation. At that stage, the oblong image I had been looking through was completely covered by a reddish coloured liquid. There was a small amount of light getting through the top, bottom and sides of this oblong shape. Although I was frightened out of my mind, that tiny speck of light gave me hope, because I wasn't in total darkness. The brain began to send comforting signals, what was happening might be temporary. With my eyes closed, I washed my face. I knew that this tragedy was happening to me and help was needed fast. Because there was no pain the experience was difficult to understand and hard to take in. Filled with fear I shouted for my wife, who was in the garden tending to the plants, "Call for a taxi I need to go to the hospital". The hysterical sound of my voice sent her running up the stairs, frightened out of her mind; not knowing what to expect. She keeps asking what is wrong. I tried to explain but she didn't understand because there were no signs of cuts or bumps. Nervously she dialed the taxi while trying to bring an air of calm into the terrifying situation. Frantically she closed the windows and doors, leaving a note for the children. In that short time I feel drained and mentally exhausted. The taxi arrived and off we went to the hospital. As we drove along, the wind pressure from the open car window enabled me to judge the distance to the hospital. Knowing the route we were taking, I could tell where we were by the bends in the road. There was a decrease in wind pressure as we passed buildings opposite open spaces. Deep in thought, I tried to analyze what had happened, while burning questions about my lifestyle invaded my brain. Was I ever going to see my family again, especially my grand-daughter? Thoughts raged chaotically through my head fuelled by a mountain of anxieties. As we got closer and closer to the hospital my eye become heavy. From pressure caused by the bleeding that was taken place. Positive thinking went through the window and negativity began to take control. Life as I knew it was over, gone with my vision, robbed by the darkness. It was only a matter of time before the doctors sealed my fate. The usual calm of the hospital corridors was absent this time. I had glimpses of images, as though in a trance, as the squeaking wheels of hospital beds and the echo of footsteps sounded in the passageways as the distant call for "Dr James" came over the PA system. It was by no means a busy night. Few doctors roamed the isles, but the speedy overcompensation of my auditory and olfactory senses did not help to alleviate my fears.

Panic and desperation laid siege to me by the fitful tension of the eye. The doctor's hands probed, while a dark abyss stood between my family and me. This was so frustrating. Only small flashes of light and fleeting glimpses of images were all I had. The "doc" spoke and I could almost feel my wife's fear as she listened anxiously for news. I wasn't too optimistic, but I was concerned about what had caused the hemorrhage in my eye. I had so many questions about how I was going to get around, and even worse, how would I carry on with the business that had been successfully growing over the years.

The disaster took place on a Sunday a day when most doctors and specialists were off for the weekend. What chance would I have seeing one of them that night? There were doctors on duty taking turns with the examination. But no one had the experience to deal with my condition there and then. The initial sessions of poking and squeezing came to an end with a decision to send me to the eye unit. I grasped desperately at optimism that something was being done. I hoped someone at the eye unit would be able to shed some light on my situation or at least give me an answer that I could understand.

At the unit, my condition was new to most of the doctors on duty, so ironically once again my condition was a spectacle generating a lot of interest. Waiting for a specialist's attention, I panicked again; the small amount of light penetrating the parameter became less. My surroundings were blurring into a thick fog. Someone had to guide me wherever I went. Having been taken from one examination room to another by different doctors, I became aware of instinctively using my ears and feet as substitutes for my eyes. It was remarkable, the speed with which my body adapted to the changes.

Sitting almost motionless while only an occasional word was spoken caused my patience to wear thin. I had been waiting around between two hospitals for seven and half-hours. It was approaching 11 p.m. and I had no clear knowledge, of what was to happen to me. With nothing interesting to stimulate the brain, my mind had a field day worrying about everything, and the more I worried the worse the fear of darkness became. By this time, my daughter and granddaughter had received the message. Arriving at the hospital frightened and exhausted, they gently caressed my face, while I could sense the erratic thumping of their hearts and trembling hands. In disbelieve and sorrow they tried to comfort my broken spirit. Angelique, my granddaughter, oblivious to the seriousness of the circumstances relieved my suffering. Her infectious laughter and playful gestures were the lifeline that held me suspended above the gaping abyss of despair and depression, which loomed beneath me.

That lonely waiting made me feel as though I hadn't had a life prior to that day. The doctor sent me home till the following day with no medication but a recommendation for total rest. Obscurity provided a blanket to hide the faces of my wife and children, but the unhappy sound of their voices allowed me to understand how they were feeling. Like me they were worried about the unknown. Those vibrations brought extreme depression, so that I wept inside. Life seemed to be over and I was doomed.

I went home in agony from the various examination techniques different doctors applied. The penetrating lights and bleeding had left my eye feeling blown up like a balloon and ready to explode. The pain and its discomfort rendered me restless, enduring a sleepless night. It was as if the entire world was against me. I felt besieged. With no experience of this kind of behaviour, I found it difficult to explain the way I felt.

A few days passed since the calamity. A typical day carried many challenges that required physiological adjustments. I could no longer wake with a calm and steady attitude to the day's activities; instead I was preparing for battle.

Starting from the basics: I slipped down stairs, popped into the bathroom, or "just" wandered off to the kitchen for a glass of milk. Such exercises were no longer simple, but had become laborious, demanding careful detailed attention and lots of determination to prevent further accidents. My feet became a battle ramp, colliding with the furniture. Independence was my objective; so I was driven by an obsessive quest to conquer what had become an alien word. Or, at the very least, I needed to successfully negotiate obstacles. However the pain and torture that ensued often left me disheartened. I would angrily drift into self-pity. Still I kept trying. Restructuring the use of my hands, feet, and ears was vital to the every day activities. Channeling my efforts into adopting new ways of coping helped to fill the voids. But, even so I wreaked havoc with so many objects in my path.

Strong will and determination helped me to develop extra sensitivity with hearing and sound, helping me to accept the situation. Turning from self-pity life became tolerable, submitting to the hand I had been dealt. Money was no help in making me feel better, nor did it restore my sight during the days of uncertainty. Wealth without health was no comfort, a lesson I will never forget.

My business with all its potential, our holiday plans, our possessions, all took second place in my thoughts. Neglect began to take its toll on the once-successful business, now literally falling apart. I was about to be left with nothing. My financial world was collapsing. Surrounded by chaos I should have been at my wits end worrying about my situation. What was I going to do? How could I maintain my comfortable lifestyle? Strangely, that wasn't the case; money, the business, wealth, and position were of no importance at the time. A fulfilling life *with vision* is what I needed. Money was useless when I could not see to spend it.

Overwhelmed by tremendous feelings of gratitude for the joy and blessing of the support from family and friends, I relied on their constant reassurance and understanding to teach me the true meaning of care. I often wonder what my life would have been without them. Catherine, my wife, adjusted her schedule to fit my needs. She was religiously cleaning up after I spilled something or knocked it over.

My daughter, Andrea, was fantastic. She tempered the fears that built-up inside; while my granddaughter Angelique created a diversion for my thoughts. Catherine, Andrea and Angelique took turns in making sure I didn't step out of line and do things I wasn't supposed to do. Angelique was a real character. She was almost like the author of a storybook who was acting out the story. At two years of age, she knew I couldn't get around on my own. Taking hold of my hand she pulled me along like a rag doll wherever she wanted me to go. That little girl was both a tonic and an inspiration for my recovery.

A typical day began at eight o'clock in the morning. I would check my blood sugar level, and have the first of my two insulin injections per day, then I would bathe the eye and insert the first drops of my three each day. With so much to do I grew tense and my sugar levels fluctuated. That sequence continued for a long time. Andrea, God bless her, helped me to bathe the eye and apply the drops. For that I will always be grateful to her.

Andrea was the first child by my first wife who divorced me after twenty years of marriage. She had been nursing since she left school, and also had many years experience of caring for people like me. Suddenly being put in a position of having to care for her dad with all the emotional consequences might have become a drain on her sensitivity. But she was marvelous; her bubbling sense of humor, her gentle methods in making me relax left me with a feeling of guilt, knowing that I have taken the wonderful qualities she possessed for granted. Her actions taught me a lesson to appreciate all she did and how she carried out those duties.

On some days my confidence would be shattered as I failed to devise new ways of getting things done. Frustration turned my mind towards depression, and that has made me a very difficult person to understand. But Angelique was always getting up to her little tricks, which diverted my attention, as if she were aware of my feelings. Her actions were guaranteed to make me laugh.

I had to take shock of the situation and make an objective assessment of my future. The shock was difficult and too horrendous to neatly parcel and put away. Helpless, dejected and feeling useless, with plenty of time to dwell on these negative feelings I found the Christian values that I absorbed during my childhood were a tremendous boost to my beleaguered life. I was thankful to my persistent parents. My regular attendance at Church and Sunday school strengthened my belief in God and in the power of goodness.

The question was how practical was the help my faith would give me? When things went wrong comfort came in the discipline my parents exercised. One of their ways in which they coped was through praying: they would pray more often than normal. Surprisingly, for reasons I could never understand, their problems would disappear in a short time. Soft as it may seem, I was convinced that praying was the right thing to do. I was sure their prayers were answered in many ways. It seemed logical to me to accept that if God answered their prayers then he would answer mine. As devoted Christians my parents were constantly praying to God, which left an indelible impression on me becoming a source of strength. In my world of darkness, as I talked to God, I did not and could not speak aloud. That could easily be misconstrued as the first stage of madness. Quietly I would remove all negative thoughts and allow my body to relax. Slowly I would drift into a world of calm and tranquility.

As a child I was constantly reassured that every problem could easily be sorted out, if I believed and prayed to God. During those dark days I put my parents' advice to the test. What after all did I have to lose? How worse could it become? So at this time of tribulation in my life, I prayed more frequently, but also differently. Less emphasis was put on specific requests; instead I thanked God for allowing me to have gone so long without having a major incident. Praying like this left me with a feeling of calm and a strange sense of foreboding as I waited without knowing what I was waiting for. This attitude has nothing to do with being soft, or becoming a 'goody-goody' person, as many often perceive Christians to be. Although it was only a few days since I had become ill – I was lonely. My Christian upbringing taught me tolerance, which played a crucial role in my recovery. It gave me something other than the doctors to believe in, and encouraged me to be humble and pleasant, during the difficult and emotional days. The discipline developed from praying gave me the strength I needed.

My mother lived thousands of miles across the Atlantic, in New York. Although she wasn't keeping the best of health, she had to be told of my illness. Consideration of her health had to be taken in preventing her from becoming too upset and possibly breaking down. Again I became depressed as the time to phone her drew near. I knew she would be devastated by the news and

I worried more about her feelings than my own. I remember she had a similar experience when I was a child and this would reawaken the anguish she had suffered. I needed the family to help her to stay calm when she was told.

Thousands of miles away from my mother, there was I with no vision even to get to the bathroom without a struggle. My fear about my mother's reaction to my news was that of a ten-year old child, rather that of a fifty-five-year-old man. I wondered why that was. However hard I try to solve this puzzle, the answer remains the same. It stemmed from the Christian teachings instilled in me. Finally I plucked up the courage to phone and tell her the news in chapter and verse. I spoke to her, pausing for a minute, as I waited for that dreaded moment when her voice became soft and quiet, and her tears flowed, but surprisingly, she showed more courage than I expected. Stress gave way to relief; the pressure had gone. But there where other things to worry about.

Decision day arrived in the form of a very important hospital appointment. The specialists were due to decide the type of treatment I should have. There was also a chance of hearing what had caused the bleeding. Filled with apprehension about the visit, I hoped for good news. But what would have pleased me most, would be learning what was wrong and if they could rectify the problem, even if it didn't lead to an immediate cure. As we traveled to the hospital, the thought of judgement day finally looms. When I arrived my attendance was registered with the charge nurse and in a short time I was called to begin the tests. Once again, there were a number of doctors on duty, and each one ready to have a look into my eye. I was treated with more intensity than sympathy. Discussing their findings among themselves, leaving me unable to see their faces, they did not seem to understand what was going on. Although I could hear their voices clearly, I could not understand the medical jargon. They had left me to wait and wait, while I had to endure the pain from the 'on and off' marathon of bright lights used during the examination. Frustrated from the lack of information, I found it hard to believe that the doctors knew what the problem was. They could not agree on the best course of action. The hours of decision making finally ended. They decided to let nature do the job, sending me home to rest for a few days. By that time they said that there should be clear signs of an improvement, and more important, it should be enough time for the bleeding to stop.

Once at home, I took the instruction to rest seriously. I took control of the settee, allowing those soft inviting cushions to caress my body. But even among the comfort of those cushions strange thoughts shadowed my horizon. The specialist had not said I was going to be blind but the feeling that it was not good news sparked an overwhelming fear, that I would be. Uncertainty stalked my thoughts. I took advantage of peaceful moments to pray to God for help in finding that someone, somewhere, with the knowledge and experience to deal with my situation would come forward.

I spent a number of hours in the waiting-rooms with patients suffering from similar visional problems as myself. I could not avoid listening to their anxieties. My wife and I soon became involved in conversations that exposed their sufferings of long and short-term blindness. They all had a wealth of knowledge, which they were happy to pass on. What they said gave me some understanding of what it meant to be totally blind and how it felt to have a little hope of recovery. I began to prepare for blindness. I was fortunate to have family and friends whose constant care and attention helped me through the lonely times. It wasn't loneliness from the absence of people. It was a different kind from being unable to see the expressions on people's faces or their body language, or to take part in sighted activities. At those times the imagination took over leaving me with feelings of insecurity about people's real intentions and their sincerity.

The disaster created a knock-on effect to my health. I am a diabetic and the shock of bleeding triggered off a rise in my blood sugar levels. I realised that the diabetes was the triggering factor of the hemorrhage, and it contributed to the delay in diagnosis. Extra care then had to be taken with my diet and general activities. I faced a double problem; keeping myself calm while dealing with a strictly controlled diet and dealing with all the implications of my condition.

Days slowly turned to nights and minutes crawled to hours, with no positive improvement. All my senses were put into action in developing an alternative approach. First I listened to various noises. I tried to separate the difference between sounds, differentiating bumps from screeches, pinpointing their places of origins. I carefully analysed them until I was sure of the direction the sounds were coming from to fill my lonely days and help me to identify the difference between the wind blowing against the door and someone trying to open it.

When the time came for my next appointment with the specialist, I was nervous about reliving the first painful examinations. I became hesitant and anxious. But this appointment was going to be quite different. Pictures of the inner eye were going to be taken that day which would allow the specialist to assess the extent of the damage, and work out the best and safest way of carrying out the treatment. A dye was injected into the vein of my arm which would flow through to the vein of my eye. Pictures were taken in an attempt to show the position of the leak. That session was so risky and intense that a doctor and a nurse were in attendance throughout. I was glad when it was over, it was much, much worse than I expected. The camera light was painful and I became wary of examinations and the doctors who did them. By the time I had left hospital my fear had turned to terror. During the journey I questioned myself, I was trying to find someone or something to blame. I had to finish on answers; I needed certainty. Reminding myself of the misfortune I suffered in my childhood didn't help either. But as I thought about my Christian beliefs, one incident stood out.

Dad was a farmer, a very strong man, of medium build who talked to the cows and treated them like humans. One day he fell and broke his shoulder while tending to his animals. I was a child but I took notice of his actions, the way he put the pain aside and took control of his life as husband, father and provider for the family. I also listened to him praying. First he would pray for forgiveness, and then for the strength to bear the pain and finally for God's healing powers to penetrate and make his shoulder better.

Well, even though I am a grown man I did same, hoping to have the same result or almost. By the time we got home I was tired and exhausted. On the doorstep, my wife pushed the key into the lock of the beautifully varnished mahogany door that effortlessly swings open, releasing the pine fragrance of the furniture polish. She escorted me safely to a chair. A knock on the door signals the approach of visitors. Leaving the hospital in pain, and feeling sorry for myself is not the best time to be civil. Still the visitors were invited in, and made welcome. I told them of my condition, explaining the procedure the specialist had put me through. Sympathy flowed from the sound of their voices while we drank tea and talked. Within a short time my pain suddenly disappeared. I am not saying that it was my praying that did it, but I was sure the pain went as suddenly as it came and that abruptness left me wondering.

Accepting my situation of blurred vision with the intention of retaining some sort of independence meant continuous practicing, which caused mayhem in doing anything at all in what seemed to me to be a smoke-filled room. I was a one-man show, my performance was equal to Laurel and Hardy rolled into one and it wasn't funny ha-ha. Time seemed to move quickly as my techniques become more skillful. But, the family wasn't amused with some of the things I did, which made them nervous so that they spoke to me harshly. After all they were very protective of me, and they knew that a fall could cause permanent damage.

I started to understand more about my eye, which created a great deal of interest with entertaining moments. This was amusement at its best, just what I needed to distract attention from the seriousness of the situation. Whenever I would try to focus on something, I would see the mountain of reddish fluid inside my eye. My entertainment came from the movement of the fluid as it flowed in the opposite direction to the movement of my head. For instance, if I bent my head downwards the fluid flowed upwards. If I lifted my head, the fluid would then flow down. Yet, I could not see to pick up a glass from the table without knocking it over. Out would go my hand toward the glass or cup, but my fingers would knock it over, spilling all the contents. It was as frustrating for the family and humiliating for me.

At first the movement of the fluid in the eye was disturbing, but after playing with its magical displays, I became mesmerized and more relaxed. What was spooky, no other person could see those 'pictures'. Explaining them to members of the family was difficult, because they thought I wasn't telling the truth. Furthermore they could not see it, or could they? Was it too disturbing to acknowledge?

There was so much to learn, leaving me to wonder how on earth I managed to find my way around during those turbulent days without injuring myself more. The family paid extra attention to my safety. They saw the need that for me to retain some kind of independence. Even though I knew my surroundings, it was a struggle getting about. I could not identify objects on the floor. It was a regular occurrence to trip over the cat which scarred me out of my mind, even to the point of swearing, but not in a vulgar way of course.

Things I had taken for granted while my vision was intact became important safety devices for my existence. Even now, I always maintain a cautious approach to the things I do, whether simple or difficult. Stuck in a world of darkness, I felt as though I had never slept, and I had the nagging thought that I seemed always to be awake. Filled with nervous anticipation, I had to go back to the hospital. The specialist was going to reveal the results of those photographs. Held tight by the arms of my wife on one side and daughter on the other, I was taken along a maze of hospital corridors. I felt safe with them, yet frightened still. Noises sounded louder than before. The place was extremely busy, with people and equipment moving in all directions. The journey to the waiting room seemed endless. My escorts were pulling me from one side to the other to avoid the comers. The doctors examined the pictures and conferred for a long time, but they finally came to a conclusion and made their diagnosis.

They decided to put me through a course of laser treatments, which would extend over a period of weeks until the offending clot had cleared. The aim was to remove all the small veins at the back of the eye, which if successful would halt the bleeding and stop any future occurrence. That was great news; something was being done at last. I was nervous but convinced the treatments would eventually cure my condition. That news was the best so far. For the first time I went through an examination without pain. My relaxed state was shared by the whole family, although I could not see the expressions on their faces, I sensed their feelings and I knew how they felt. We went home filled with relief and hope.

As a mobile catering operator covering a large area of the town, I was known and liked by all kinds of people. As news of my plight filtered out it wasn't long before I was swamped with concerned inquires and visitors. But although I appreciated their concern, continually repeating my story became exhausting, and it grew worse as the number of visitors daily increased. Catherine had her hands full; not only had she to care for me but she had to struggle with her mother who lived a hundred yards from our house and was also ill at the same time. She had to juggle her time between me and her mother and that was not easy for her.

# Chapter 2

# FRIEND

Throughout my life I have had many good friends. Adulthood and the responsibilities that go with it send us in different directions to forge our own destinies. But, this can leave a vacuum of loss, with surprising results, as in my case. Among my friends was one so honest, so cool and helpful in every way. His name was "Benji". I will forever be in his debt. Benji was a Jamaican, who travelled to the UK in the late fifties. He was five years my senior, a steel erector, tough on the outside but soft and gentle as a lamb. During his visits we talked about everything except my blindness. Benji would play records, and take me for long walks to reminisce about the old days. And, if that wasn't enough, we would take the mickey out of each other as we had always done over the years. Benji would wind me up listening to my problems with that chuckling laugh. He was my escort on many visits to the doctors and trips into town, keeping me in touch with the real world. He literally stopped me from vegetating.

After the second laser treatment, which did not show any signs of a quick fix, I was forced to confront a mountain of doubts and the old flame of self-pity was ready to ignite. However, soon there were two people on my case, Angeleque and Benji, whose determination made sure I was brought back into line, giving me some zest for life. Benji's funny jokes and Angeleque's awkward questioning press my conversion button and douse the flame of doubts. How wonderful it is to have families and friends like mine in times of desperation.

I was given a treatment program, which if followed should help to rebuild my confidence in my approaches. Positive thinking was my goal, kicking negative thoughts to touch.

Before the tragedy, occasionally friends who were having hard times with an illness and finding it difficult to confide in their families would seek my advice. I would try to be objective because that, I believe, encourages the individual to share their concerns with their family. How shortsighted I was. The table has turned and I was caught in the same spiral web. But it wasn't easy to carry out my own advice. Burdening my kids with a problem that would cause misery to themselves and others was the last thing I wanted to happen. On the children's visits, they would tell me jokes and keep me up to date with the latest gossip, which was enough to keep my mind occupied for a short spell. It also helped to make the days pass without worrying about my incapacity. My entertainment was big news and most exciting. I would seize opportunities to tell them in graphic detail of the magical pictures playing in my eye. 'They are spectacular', I claimed and 'the experiences are enjoyable'.

I would talk about my feelings, but never overstep the boundary by allowing them to know what was really going through my mind. Gently I would gloss over the rest, leaving it for another day. The parents who can allow their children to express their thoughts and wishes get my admiration. I suppose that's what many describe as 'closeness within the family', a practice I applaud and respect. In my experience, it is what most families dream of. Unfortunately, I was blessed with just the ordinary independent individual thinkers, who liked to work out their own problems wherever possible. But I accept them as they are and don't regret the failure to develop that special bond.

I would hate to leave the perception that we were not a close family, for of course we were. I suppose we just weren't one of those rear-bonded families who always do everything together. Grownups are responsible for their actions, whether they are from the bonded, or the close independent families. A very fascinating subject for future discussion!

There was a marked improvement after five days treatment; I had seen the inside of my eye, which was at first frightening but at the same time fascinating. This meant that there was vision in the eye, but something was blocking its path. The inner eye takes on the same layout as a city street map, with two or three motorways running through. To obtain those pictures, I would position myself as close as possible to a low-voltage light bulb, to the point where the heat is about to set the eye alight. A picture would then emerge on the closest clear surface that was in front or wherever I was focusing at the time. Trapped light inside the eye projected pictures of its layout, creating a hole the size of a ten-pence piece, with everything around it foggy. This magical sideshow diverted my thoughts and relaxed my body allowing time to slip by. This new phenomenon induced hope and confidence that one day soon some vision would return. It also provided me with a ready-made topic for conversation and I would use every opportunity to talk about it, boring the pants off visitors.

Those early days saw an array of different appointments that had to be kept, which being a good boy, I did. The taxis were regular callers at my door. Not all were to the hospitals or to the doctors. My condition dictated that I could not return to work in the immediate future. All I could do was register long-term unemployed. But doing that was depressing, bringing on feelings of lack of self worth. I knew I had done well but to go from this to helplessness within five weeks was devastating. However, even amidst those anguished times there was laughter. Getting into a taxi often created humorous results. Normally a person would enter a car sideways in a sitting position, the bottom reaches the seat, the legs are lifted and placed into the car to finish the movement. The trouble was, I could not carry out the manoeuvre. Disoriented from the blindness I could not tell my right from my left or where I was going. So, entering the car I would step forward the same as boarding a bus. One thing stands out; someone would put his or her hand on my head to stop it banging on the roof. What is funny about it? We have often seen on television, during a cops-and-robbers program, a police person using their hands to protect the heads of detainees. The reality of being a prisoner was never far from my thoughts, especially when things weren't going according to plan. The drivers knew me well and would put an extra effort into safeguarding my sensitivity.

# Chapter 3

# PANIC

Weeks later and yet another appointment, which would determine whether the treatments were working and if there was any improvement. I was in a relaxed frame of mind looking forward to hearing some good news. Having arrived at the waiting room, I sat for a few minutes before being called to the examination room by the specialist. 'Sit down', 'Chin placed on the chest', 'Eyes open', the light switches on and another examination was in full swing. The pain wasn't as intense as it had been before, so when he said 'finished', I was still feeling comfortable. He pushed back his chair and began to explain his findings. I could feel the warmth of his smile setting my body aglow. He said. "I have good news at last. The bleeding has stopped, but it still leaves a clot in the shape of a mushroom hanging in the path of your vision". That's dangerous in his estimation. He continues, "There are only so many laser treatments you can have, and it will not remove the offending clot."

At that moment, my bottom sank into the chair, the good news appeared as well as the bad news. My brain began to fry; confusion became the order of the day. Trying to listen to him was hopeless. I could hear his voice in the distance, which made it impossible to understand what he was saying. I wasn't doing a good job of it. But in my confused state of mind, I would not forget his words endlessly ringing through my ears like a continuous musical note. He said, "You have two choices: colour surgery, which will take longer, but would stop you from going blind, or pray for a miracle". What was worse, neither him nor his colleagues in that hospital were equipped to carry out that type of operation. The doctor began mapping out what he thought would be the best way forward. "What we have to do is find you the best surgeons in the country who have experience with diabetic conditions," he said in a soft and reassuring voice, trying to put my mind at ease. He browsed through the register searching for what he wanted. He sounded wonderful, but I was shaking on the inside, because my world was once again turned upside down.

It had been eleven weeks since the accident, and time was running out fast; any treatment taken was now extremely urgent. The doctor and his staff spent hours on frantic telephone calls alerting three different hospital doctors who specialized in my condition trying to secure an appointment. After a few hours there was a result. He procured the services of a specialist whom he knew and trusted to do the job. All I had to do was to sit back and wait for the call.

The delays had pushed my situation into a critical stage. It was getting toward the end of the year, with Christmas holidays looming and possibly causing more delays. My condition began to worsen. It was time to get the family doctor more involved. His gentle persuasion secured an appointment immediately after the Christmas holidays, five months since that dreadful day! Throughout those weeks my mind was in limbo. I was on the verge of accepting blindness, because there seemed to be no alternative. Some days I would reinforce my positive attitude of being strong, and other days I could not stop the surge of depression. No matter what the family did to cheer me up, nothing worked. I was going through a phase of depression which sometimes lasted between two to three hours. The light that was getting into the eye began to fade, turning hope into despair. I was frightened that the inevitable was about to manifest itself and total blindness was only a matter of time. Nervously, I decided to send for my mother, whom I love very much, before I become totally blind.

The days were fully occupied perfecting my co-ordination, while the realities of my future became more challenging. To break the cycle Benji took me for a walk into the town, where I seized the opportunity to buy mother's flight ticket. Having an imminent flight date would be exciting for her, and I needed her like a child. I was very happy when she arrived, even though I could not see her, but sensed her only as a shape in a smoke-filled room. But the sound of her voice was enough to calm my fears.

Her room had been prepared at the top of the first-floor stairs over-looking the front of the house. A television set had been provided in case she needed to be on her own. Although I was very anxious to have her with me I was still very anxious about the effect that my condition would have on her. But I needn't have worried. She was able to accept it and was happy to be with me, sharing some laughter with the rest of the family. I knew there was nothing she could do that would guarantee a speedy recovery, but her mere presence made a difference to the atmosphere within the family. It also helped to reduce the burden on my wife and children. Her presence during those four weeks brought out the best in everyone, family and friends alike. She was good at highlighting the funny side of a problem or setback, turning it into a comedy. She also attracted extra visitors to the house, bringing more fun and laughter.

Adapting my hearing to work like radar, I could separate sounds and match them to individuals or objects. I knew when mother left the room and crept up the stairs. I could detect vibrations whether they came from the wind or individuals. One day shortly after my mother arrived, she crept upstairs and shut the door behind her. Curious movements, I felt my way to her room and knocked. I opened the door and stepped inside. To my surprise she was praying with a lot of passion. My intrusion disgusted me – I can't explain why. But hearing her pray reassured me. She was dealing with the situation the best way she knew.

Stories from my childhood brought laughter to the family, reminding them of funny moments, even though they were a bit embarrassing to me. Worst of all, I could not see their faces. I love and will always miss my Mother's resilience, her modern and free spirit, her positive outlook and the way she could create a party atmosphere. My grandmother had brought her up during the war, when my mother had saw life change so radically for so many people. She married at an early age, and with an eye for fast growth and eager to increase the population she and her husband produced eleven children in twenty-four years. There were four girls and seven boys. Unfortunately one of the girls died as a baby and the second boy-child of the family died at nine years of age. The second baby died tragically in his late twenties. As poor parents they knew what it meant to be fraught with disappointment and despair. My mother had seen and helped in many disastrous situations and she developed the qualities to deal with my condition. Her fun loving character soon spilled over into her surroundings, and infected me as well.

Her return to the brothers and sisters I longed to be with left gaping holes in my life for a long time. I wanted to pack my bags and go with her, but unfortunately that wasn't practical. Towards the end of her stay I gained more confidence than I imagined. I stopped wearing shoes or slippers in the house, which helped me to find my way around much easier. It also improved my balance, making me more sensitive to the space around me. My only discomfort was putting up with banging my toes against objects. But gradually as my toes became more sensitive, I could use them to detect and retrieve small objects from the floor.

Without vision to guide them my fingers became clumsier than normal, so I used my toes to locate objects on the floor, which my finger had difficulty finding. It was not always an easy option, because my feet had their fair share of bumps and bruises. Extra care had to be taken when carrying out those manoeuvres because of my diabetes. The smallest injury could become major if it were to become infected. After my mother left I was a very miserable person. For a few days my heart sank in despair, desperate for reassurance that I would be cured or at least that I would regain some vision.

Out of the blue, an old friend, Danny, turned up. It would have been twenty-five years since I had last seen him. Separated when we left high school, and now here he was. We had known each other since junior school and had been best buddies during those years. People mistook us for brothers. Our behavior was like that of twins. The joy of meeting him again was difficult to hide, though I was puzzled about his sudden appearance, wondering which one of the family had told him about my situation. Danny was one of those people who would never say die. For him there was always an explanation for everything. We were the same age, but he was plumper, especially around the waistline. He had always been a cocky fellow, who insisted on being right. The kids at school called him 'Mister Know it-all'.

No sooner Danny waltzed through the door than he began to impose himself on the family. He started advising me on all the things I would have to do to help me through my illness. Feeling downtrodden with mother absent and not being able to see the man while he continued to cloud the room with his know-it-all philosophy, I was fuming with anger. After all, I had not seen the man for years and suddenly he appeared telling me what, how, and when to do things in my home. He was being downright offensive.

What came next was astonishing. As suddenly as Danny entered our lives upsetting the balance we had been trying to attain, he picked the telephone up to ring his friend, a therapist, to ask him to come and speak with me. Listening to him, I was flabbergasted by his cheek. I was in no position to be rude to him, so patiently I waited for an explanation, but none came. I could only sit preparing myself for the unexpected. Within about an hour there was a knock on the door. It was Danny's friend. I was amazed, but reluctantly found myself respecting him more. For all his domineering ways he had some fine qualities. I found myself admiring him.

Danny's friend, Mr. Hunt, a therapist, who worked for the Blind Society for a number of years, was well aware of my predicament. The unexpected visitors made all the family nervous because neither Danny nor his friend had ever been to my home making them total strangers to the family, plus the room was crowded. Benji, Andrea, Angelique, Catherine and myself with Danny and his friend, Mr. Hunt, made the room hot and noisy. Catherine and Andrea got busy, making us all tea, while Angeleque did her usual job of interrogating everyone. The questions she asked should have been reserved for grown ups only. Nevertheless, after constant nagging from her mother, she allowed us a bit of space to talk.

The therapist seemed to be very knowledgeable with far-reaching experience. He explained his experience with patients who had similar conditions to mine, and he told me how he helped with their problems by teaching them ways to cope and overcome difficulties, helping to make their lives interesting and fulfilling. In short he showed me how to accept my situation and how I could motivate myself to make changes. We talked for half an hour, while Danny and the others drank tea in the kitchen. During that time he gave me a better understanding of what I could do, and I left ashamed of being so judgmental towards Danny. Mr. Hunt and Danny restored my failing confidence. "If the worst comes about", Mr. Hunt said, "there are programs available especially adapted for your survival".

Angelique became fidgety as her bedtime drew near. Benji was also feeling the effects of a long day and decided to go home. I thought Danny and Mr. Hunt would leave as well. Instead Mr. Hunt went to his car very quickly without saying much; I had no idea of the seriousness of what he was about to do. Returning to the room he said, "Right your first job is to make a cup of tea." It took a few minutes of practice to make that cup of tea. "It isn't a competition so relax and take your time", said Mr. Hunt. Soon I conquered the fears of tipping hot water over others and myself. I was soon feeling quite confident as well as extremely grateful to Mr. Hunt and Danny.

When Mother returned home she telephoned to let us know that she was safe. I could here the anxiety in her voice, disguised by her chuckles, but I was able to reassure her with good news. She would hear the new optimism in my voice. Christmas was coming, she reminded me, and that will give everyone something to think about.

The fast approaching holidays put an end to the laser treatment and also to the magical display of fluid, though my sight hadn't improved. That mushroom shaped clot was still blocking out my vision. For the first time in many years I was compelled to do nothing in the preparation for Christmas and I felt quite inadequate. I have always been actively involved in the Christmas preparations, offering both suggestions and practical help. But this year, all the organizing and preparing gifts for everyone was left to Catherine. I could only sit and listen. The decoration of various colored stencils and lights transformed the house, making the place sparkle, giving a new meaning to my magic show. With all the fluid drained away, the eye become more susceptible to low-voltage lights and their position near me. Allowing the light to engulf my eye would project a beautiful array of colourful pictures repeating experiences I had with the fluid movements. Hours were spent testing its strength, resurrecting hope for what I thought was lost. I invited Catherine to enjoy the show, but I was unaware that she could not see what I was watching. Even though I encouraged her, it was useless, and again I felt foolish.

My biggest problem was bedtime. Getting to sleep was difficult whether I closed my eye or not. I was in a world of continual darkness. Yet my brain was firing on all cylinders, sleeping was not on its agenda. But I needed to rest because it was important to maintain the continuous draining of the fluid from my eye. Some days I thought it was a waist of time getting out of bed, because no sooner was I out, I was ready to go back. These were boring days, difficult to measure – a continuous extension of the night.

Mr. Hunt's new program began show some benefits, however. I was moving around the house without inflicting injury to myself, which gave me a wonderful feeling of achievement. Thanks to the therapy program becoming successful, I was bathing without help, and applying toothpaste to the brush without causing a mess. Achieving these milestones, which most people take for granted, had one requirement.

Everything had to be kept in the same position. But, I grew more confident every day. Benji would call on the telephone daily; he would also pop in to see if I needed to go out, or just to cheer me up. I would tell him the latest development in my condition. He sometimes thought I was going mad. It took a brave person to believe my stories; they seemed so far-fetched, even to me. But I can assure you they were truthful. As time went by he took them with a pinch of salt, doing his best not to upset me. If only I could have done something to convince him.

As Christmas Day approached, Benji had a lot to talk about. The festive season was firmly underway: a drink of beer confirms it. The house was a hive of activity, as preparations were in full swing. Children and grandchildren paraded in and out, bringing and collecting gifts. I could sense and enjoy the excitement, though I could not see any faces.

Grace was too ill to leave her home, so the family arranged to spend the day with her. It would be the first year since Catherine and I had been together, that I would be unable to spend Christmas day with her. Catherine and the family would split their time between Grace and me. The holidays would never be the same again and I was helpless to do anything about it.

Sitting comfortably in my chair, I allowed my thoughts to cascade like a mountain stream. Suddenly it dawned on me, if I were totally blind, what could I do to maintain some sort of productive life? I would never want to sit around doing nothing, but what kind of job could I do? Perhaps I knew that this wasn't the time for such questions. I tried to leave them for the future. I could work on that problem then.

Christmas Day came and went with all plans falling into place. The phone rang many times with messages from mother, children, family and friends. Exchanging of gifts, music and laughter, excitement among the little ones. The weatherman predicted a dry day, while the bookmakers challenged punters to bet on snow for the day.

The day seemed to go quicker than it came. I was left on my own for a short time. The excitement had died down, the children have had than enough to eat, and they left only empty boxes and screwed up wrapping paper. I didn't want to experience another Christmas like that again. For once I wanted to go to bed.

My long-awaited appointment was fast approaching, and I was never more nervous. My condition was desperate and there was no guarantee that the city hospital specialist could successfully repair the damage to my eyes. There were lots of encouraging messages from family and friends, but nothing strong enough to take away my anxiety.

Angeleque and her mother arrived bringing most of her presents to show me, even though I could not see them. They gave her something extra to talk about. As soon as the car pulled up at the gate, her voice would let me know who it was. Having her around pushes gloomy thoughts away. Around Angelique, everyone sat up and took notice!

My first appointment was at the city hospital, 147 miles from home, or two-and-a-half hours by train, and three hours by road. The area was strange to me, and made worse because I could not see. However after having made that journey several times, the city landmarks were vivid in my memory. They hadn't changed and I had a mental picture of where I was. My eldest son Carl and his wife Sandra decided to take me by car. An early start was essential, and as usual I prayed that the good Lord would guide us throughout the journey, and hopefully give a fruitful result to the examination. But my greatest wish was to have an assurance from the specialist that I would have some sight again. That would be music to my ears. Early morning and the journey begin. I was about to hear my fate. I was terrified of what the specialist might find. As usual my brain was working overtime trying to solve problems. I thought of everything that could go wrong, building up an enormous mountain of tension. I was crying, the inside of my mouth became dry, I needed to use the bathroom, but when we stopped there was no action. Nervousness was dictating how I felt – a mess – reaching breaking point – only screaming could make anyone understand what was happening to me. Thank goodness! Had those thoughts continued I would probably have had a heart attack. The sudden jolt put things into perspective and I cheered up. Congestive traffic slowed us down and created anger and frustration around the drivers. It wasn't difficult for me to tell that we were in the heart of the city. If only I could see, how easy it would have been to help them navigate! The whizzing cars sent a pollulated, yet cooling breeze through the slightly open window, giving a fresh feeling against my face. I was in silence now. Catherine became concerned, she began explaining where we were and what landmark we had reached. Her soft voice made me feel as if was seeing everything for myself. I wanted to be closer to her. My affection rose up the scale, but she is not an affectionate person. Holding her hand in silent communication was rare, but necessary to our relationship. In my sphere of darkness, in a world where light plays the most important part, it was difficult to avoid negative thoughts. Holding her hands was a signal for attention. If she failed to respond within a reasonable time, I would interpret her response that something was wrong, and I would grow anxious.

Carl gently pushed along with the stop-and-start traffic. His wife Sandra was doing an excellent job of navigating. Her positive communication skills made the journey easy for her husband. She is a hairdresser and a beautician and always in style, and she has many fine qualities too. I liked being where we were. Enthusiasm invited me to dish out instructions, about what to look for next, pointing out the important landmarks from memory.

Pollution has become a shocking problem. Inhaling exhaust gases highlighted the fortunate position that I enjoyed, living in one of the most beautiful parts of the United Kingdom, where the air is cleaner. The disturbing behaviour of the city drivers caused Carl to complain. "Their attitude stinks", he said. They acted like the only ones who had the right to use the roads. Darting out from side streets, blowing of horns for no real reason, frightening innocent people, causing him to take evasive action, they complicated an already difficult drive. Their attitude left me wondering: could the carbon monoxide gasses be causing those flashed of impatience?

Getting to the hospital meant traveling across the city, taking in the main traffic and the most beautiful scenic parts, the Houses of Parliament and Buckingham Palace. Police on horseback with noisy hooves on the road spirit lifted my spirit. The splendour of colours mirrored the bright shining brass decorations, as onlookers cheered with delight. Carl weaved his way through the queues of taxis hustling from street to street of open buses and crowded parks, historical buildings and huge monuments with tourists taking in the view. Colourful flowerbeds surrounded by lush green lawns, hedges cut and trimmed, welcoming visitors.

I was reluctant to ask our position, but information came to me, telling me where we were. Travelling along the riverbank the memories of high tide and fresh breezes blowing the colourful boats moored on the water's edge came back to me. I saw them in my minds eye. Some of those craft were home to city workers whose family home is in the countryside, others were the only homes for their occupants, while a few were pleasure boats.

I wished I were as free as those little boats. They seemed alive, as if they played musical chairs, rolling from side to side, like birds in flight, with no worries or fear. While my brain ran riot with my fantasies, Carl reached the hospital car-park. With shaking legs, quivering lips and fragile nerves I stepped from the car. With a firm grip, I held onto Catherine arms as she gently led me from the car park, which was on the opposite side of the road from the hospital. Carl joined us at the crossing to inject his masculinity, firmly holding the other arm. Carefully escorted, I felt like an unruly child being taken to the Headmaster for punishment. The noise seemed greater than anywhere else I could remember. Cold, with a dry throat, I yearned for a warm cup of tea. As I moved towards the entrance, my heart would seem to leap to the tip of my tongue ready to pop out. The smooth pavement seemed busy with people, hurriedly pushing to pass in different directions. In a soft and gentle voice I heared the words, "Here are the rails", and automatically I grabbed hold of them.

Climbing the steps reminded me of the therapist's training, counting the number of steps, five flights of them. They were smooth, made from marble. The strong smell of cigarette smoke seemed to choke me. Carl said, "Smoking isn't allowed inside the building, so everyone smoke on the steps". I haven't smoked for a long time, and the smell gave me the urge to smoke again.

I could feel tension as Catherine took me through a double door. Reality began to overwhelm my thoughts; the search for an answer was stamped on my forehead. Invoking silly thoughts, like 'if only' which didn't help. My only hope would come from the specialist. Only then would I be a happy man. Like a lamb to the slaughter I follow the others. My hands were wet from perspiration. My fingers slowly lost their strength. Nervousness devoured me like ants on a lump of sugar. The corridor was very busy, like the hospital itself. What was disturbing was the behavior of sighted people. In a hospital that deals with people with impaired vision, it was surprising to discover how the sighted gave very little regard to patients who were nervous. Sighted

people, both workers and visitors, moved about in close prox-
imity to patients, sometimes rushing, which left me feeling intimi-
dated and lost.

We finally reach the clinic. We are asked to sit and wait.
Although it was very busy, there was an uneasy silence; you
could hear a pin drop. It was a dreadful feeling as if it were a
mortuary. While I waited and listened to the names being called
I began to count the numbers, feeling like I was being reported
to my superior and not being told why. Catherine described the
layout of the clinic while Carl quenched my thirst with a warm
refreshing drink, to calm my nerves. While I sat and waited for
my name to be called, I began to wonder how a condemned
man might feel when he waits for the judge's ruling on whether
or not he would go to jail.

There was a hot coffee in my hand when the specialist called
my name and that was a recipe for disaster. Frightened by the
sound of my name, I spilled the hot coffee over my legs. Even
though I was ready when the specialist called my name, when he
did, nervousness rapidly took over, and my bum stuck to the
chair. Although, what was comforting was that he was at the
door ready to escort me into the examination room. That was
helpful, I was glad to know that I would not struggle to find the
way. Catherine quickly took my hands to escort me to the door.
At that stage the tears were about to flow, while my knees rattled
like a loose bolt. Inside the examination room the specialist
showed me to a chair.

Applying drops to my eye, he resumed making small talk while
reading the notes. I must have been looking as I was feeling
worried. Touching my head he said, "Don't worry we'll soon put
you right". The examination began and once again the bright light
used was the same as I had experienced during the earlier
examinations. While the light penetrated deep into the eye the
magical phenomena were once again evident, and my thoughts
go into neutral. He switched off the light, indicating he was finished. For a few seconds, I had an amazing experience. I could
see the layout of the room; there were two rows of tables and
chairs, trolleys and magnifying equipment, desk with notes and

small tables, which I could not recognize. Those minutes of intense observation seemed like a lifetime. Patiently waiting to hear his result, I was sent to other departments for more tests. It felt like being in a game of pass the parcel. A few hours of marathon testing filled me with self-pity and I was in pain. The specialist talked of his findings and was pleased to confirm his suspicions. He recommended surgery as the only option, but at the same time he was reassuring. Hopefully I would be able to see as well as before.

Oh my Lord, was I hearing right? Or was he saying that to make me feel good? A million thoughts invaded my brain, please God let it be true. That quiet smooth voice would not deceive me, would it? In desperation I raised doubts about the validity of his answers. Having waited for so long, seeing so many doctors, my faith had become weak. I suppose it was a procedure he went through every day. Anyway I am sure it would have been in his interest to be truthful. Harboring negative thoughts would not have done me any good either. He asked a lot of questions, which I answered as accurately as possible. Patiently, I waited for a decision that was six months overdue.

A fire erupted in my head, my brain was alight with anxiety. In a quiet and unassuming voice, while he continued to write his notes, he said, "Come back in six weeks time". Oh my God six weeks, did I hear him right the first time? I almost wet myself with shock. He was busily preparing the admission papers needed for my return. It was upsetting because the hospital appointment had implied that I should take extra clothing in case I was to stay over, giving me the impression that I would be admitted on the same day. But, there was a consolation; the drops have given me a new lease on life, they stung at first, but they had fantastic results. There were faint images; nevertheless I could *see* something, making the disappointment a little easier to absorb. That was progress whichever way I looked at it. I decided not tell anyone while I carried a deadly secret. I left hospital with knowledge that light was getting into the eye. During the return journey, I saw flashes of light from passing cars, but that was enough to keep me buzzing with hope. No one had the faintest idea of why

I was in such a good mood, although they thought it was the result of having a date for the operation. I kept up the pretence because I had no idea how long it would last, and I could not take the chance of telling anyone in case things went back to the way they had been.

Arriving home, the fact that I could see the outline of the furniture set my soul ablaze with happiness. As the day passed the images became clearer, meaning that the deceit I was practicing became more difficult to maintain. Careful steps had to be taken in case anyone found out! I could not speak about the things I recognized because I was scared the improvement was a short-term gain or fluke. Keeping silent would avoid disappointment if the vision suddenly went into reverse.

When Andrea and Angelique visited, I had the opportunity to go for walks. I felt desperate to speak. It was impossible to avoid noticing and admiring the actions of this clever little girl. Wearing a beautiful flower-patterned frilly dress, white socks, black shoes and pink ribbons, she would look adorable. Her long curly hair was combed and parted, and in two ribbon tied the hair with bows, making her absolutely gorgeous. Looking so elegant and acting so grown up, she was instrumental in my recovery. Emotions filled my heart. I could see my granddaughter. In anticipation I pinched myself making sure I wasn't dreaming. No, I was alive and it was my little angel, not someone else's child. I experienced one of my most proud moments and I did not share it with anyone, not even her mother who deserved it most. I wished that Angeleque would be given the chance to grow up as graceful and beautiful as she looked at that moment.

Although I could only recognize individual items at close range, there was enough sight to determine shapes and their position in the room. This allowed me to get around objects, provided that I moved slowly. That put a stop to the constant bumping. It also generated a pleasant atmosphere in the house. I began to smile more and so did everyone else.

Whilst I was sighted, I could not avoid observing blind people as they went about their business. Strange, I thought, their heads were always held high towards the sky, which evoked concern to my behaviour. Worrying that I might adopt that kind of posture, making my affliction obvious to the sighted, I became conscious of my every action, constantly reminding myself of my posture, hoping to prevent everyone from treating me as if I were totally blind. I did everything I could to conceal my blindness from the sighted.

Winter days took their toll, the wind blew with a menacing force, and led into wet and unpredictable weather patterns. Catherine's days were fully stretched, doing the outdoor chores necessary to keep the house going, and taking care of her mum, but leaving me for longer periods on my own. With plenty of energy, I easily perfected my new approach to doing the things that make life more comfortable. On dry and sunny days, which were rare, the hot sunrays beamed through the window brightening up the whole household. Crowned with this jewel of a free spirit and consumed by a hunger to satisfy, I began to think of a surprise to make Catherine happy. From all the simple things I could do, I had to select cooking her a meal. I must have been utterly mad to even consider such an operation. I haven't been near the stove in over nine months, I was disorientated and I could not see my fingers in front of me. Yet I was going to cook a meal. "Oh boy!" That's my challenge I thought, so let's get on and do it. With no care for the consequences, I set out to establish for myself the position of the household appliances and food. The good news was that everything was in the same position I remembered. That was my first hurdle. I surveyed the kitchen by feeling my way around every inch of space until I was satisfied that I knew my way. The gas stove was a major problem, since I could not read the dial or see the blue flame. How on earth I was going to manage? Still, I wasn't deterred.

The next big milestone was what meal could I manage. Great news, luck was on my side, I opened the freezer, and feeling my way around, I recalled the shape of meat packages Catherine uses. I could tell whether the packages where beef, lamb, chicken or vegetables, by their shapes and sizes. Fortunately, the first package my hand could get hold of was lamb chops. I continued rummaging through the rest of the items until I found the vegetables I needed to make the meal. That was absolutely lovely! At that stage there were no thoughts of danger. They were far removed because I was on a roll, fully motivated, I had the ingredients organized and a successful meal was in the making. I selected pots and containers, lined up in easy reach. Having collected and identified all the ingredients, I set them out in order of taste, I was ready to perform what seemed an impossible task. I wish I had taken a picture of the kitchen that day to record the chaos that was being created and the dangerous position I putting the family into. I wonder what my reaction would have been if I was sighted? That to me was secondary, a meal was about to take place and nothing else mattered.

I turned the gas on low and listened to the pressure. I struck a match and bingo! A small explosion indicated the stove was alight. Now for the big test. I was confronted with a slight difficulty; how could I tell if the flame was too low or too high? In a crude and clumsy way, I held my hand near the flaming burner to feel the pressure from the heat as it penetrated my fingers. I cannot emphasize how painful it was when the heat engulfed my fingers. The severity determined the heat that was required. It was a foolhardy and dangerous operation and should never at any time be repeated. With all its discomfort, I was very pleased at my success thus far. The stove was alight and with all the pain I suffered that was the easiest part of the cooking process. Still there was no reason to be defeatist. Hooray! Dinner was on its way. Although the cooking was yet to begin, I was sure that a meal would be produced. From there on the sequence of operation just fell into place. Thank goodness, no one came to the house, so my chain of thoughts and actions was not uninterrupted.

My next challenge – how to know when things were cooked? Switching on the radio and listening for the time to be announce seemed ideal. The cooking operation began on the hour. It might seem unlikely, but I am a good cook, further more, that dish is one of my specialities which I have made many times in the past. I was well aware of the cooking times for individual portions, which allowed the operation to progress more easily than I thought.

The mess I created was beyond a joke. Had my wife walked in

during cooking she would have hit the roof in anger. Luckily, good
fortune prevailed and I was able to clean up to the best of my
ability before she returned to the surprise that awaited her. I used
the mental pictures I have to prepare the dinner. I was desperate
to prove my independence. The fact that my concentration was
not disturbed meant the operation was within my capability. Navigating my way around the hot saucepans singing to the music on
the radio, banging and burning myself (the pain was of no conse-
quence) had me on a high; the achievement was something to shout
about. If only I could have seen Catherine's face when she walked
through the door, the mess, and then the meal. But I dared not
look in her eyes in case she realized I was seeing more than what
I claimed. I wondered what she was going to say, returning home
to find her blind handsome husband suddenly preparing a meal
from scratch. All the signs tell me she will feel wonderful.

I waited for the radio announcer to tell me the time so I could
tell when the cooking would be over. There was a lot of tidying-
up to do; the place had to be restored, as near as possible to its
former state. Speed was vital. Looking through those thick foggy
surroundings it was impossible to tell whether it was being done
well, but my abilities were being tested. What was great about
it? I was happy doing it. Amidst the pandemonium came the
jingling sound of the key entering the door lock. My heart leapt
in panic. I hadn't expected her to return so quickly. The adrenaline began to flow and pumped up my body like a stuffed doll. I
tried to put the containers back in the right places. Like a bomb
blast one of the containers crashed to the floor, sending Catherine
running to kitchen. She shouts "What the bloody hell is going on
in here?" Me, I stood in the middle of the kitchen with my mouth
wide open at her untimely arrival, I suppose with a pitiful expression on my face. She saw only the mess and not the dinner. "What
on earth are you doing?" We both froze for what seemed like
hours. In a childish, pitiful and quivering voice I muttered "I am
sorry, I was cooking you a surprise dinner."

My feelings and actions became that of a ten-year-old child.
Her mood quickly changes and in a soft but stern voice she said,
"What are you trying to do?"

Oh I wish I could have seen the expression on her face. Well I had thought I was being clever, when I set out to show her my appreciation in that way. It was also important to prove that I was still capable of doing something on my own. It was a pity that she didn't see it like that. She turned my good intentions into carelessness, and emphasized the danger in what I was trying to do. My actions were stupid because I could have blown up the place with me in it. Of course she was right about the danger, it squashed my eagerness to learn and to be independent. Submitting to her judgement, left me feeling confused and selfish, as if she had been trying to tell me something in a roundabout way. Her message was that in the midst of our life, while everything was going well I became blind and if that wasn't bad enough, I was about to destroy all the things we have worked for. Her outburst convinced me I was a destructive person, which had been far from her intentions.

Her shocked reaction sent my head in a spin. I couldn't take the outburst in. Nervous and apologetic I felt as if all the lights were switched off, gone were the images, leaving a sensation speeding through an endless tunnel. I scrambled to find a chair and get out of her way. Her anger caused me to wonder what caused such a drastic change in her attitude. The disappointment in her voice alarmed me. I could not believe my ears as she continued to make me feel inadequate. I wept with regret. Oblivious to her surroundings, the cat joined in the crying, but with a difference. The tantalizing aroma of the dinner sent her crazy for food. "Well cat," I said, "we are both in the same predicament." Catherine got busy picking up the scattered containers and clearing up the spills. I bent forward to stroke the cat and calm the both of us. I left her to retreat to the sitting-room. A feeling of dejection took over my thoughts with nerve wracking results. Soon came the sound of her footsteps entering the sitting room and in a consolatory mood, realising she overstepped the mark, she asked, "What kind of meal were you trying to cook?" Disappointed and angry I answered her sharply, which was rude, but I wasn't ready to play happy families just yet.

The whole concept of our lives together from the beginning

started to flash before me, reminding me of the first time we met and the character demonstrated. What a contrast because then she was so polite, kind, gentle, and always smiling. Her big brown eyes, long curling hair, and good looks was all a joy to admire. Suddenly in a moment of madness they all disappeared for no good reason. Instinctively I was approaching a milestone and I put a label on my situation: I was surplus to requirements. I wanted to scream to make everyone understand what was happening to me. But, that would not do me any good; what was private would only become public, serving no purpose. Nothing she could do or say that evening could have restored the zeal and excitement that inspired my idea of a surprise meal, which I had felt sure she would appreciate. The aim of the meal had been to say thanks for the care she had given me, and second, to tell her about the improvement that was taking place. Her unseemly display made me want to curl up and die, which might have brought relief and happiness, because after all she was only living with half a man.

The meal was finally ready. She encouraged me to come and eat, but it was too early to pretend that I was in control. Depressed? Hell no. I was so angry, I could have walked out of the house, my problem was that I could not navigate beyond the front door. My appetite had gone.

The cat stayed loyal and appreciated the comfort I was giving, gently stroking her long, soft, fluffy fur. She turned her head so often towards my face, mewing like a musical note, as if to say "Don't stop, I love it."

Evening turned into night and Catherine recognized the damage in my situation. She forced her tongue to civility and understanding, in other words, she was being nice. Knowing I was going beyond the time when I should have eaten began to cause her concern. After all I am a diabetic and too long without food could bring on a coma. She held my hands and gently led me to the dinner table in the kitchen, where the meal was waiting. I washed my hands and before I could feel for the towel she was drying them. What a turn around.

We were about to have our meal when the doorbell rang. Surprised to have visitors at a delicate time, I went to the door to find my old friend Danny (Mr. Know-it-all). He was invited in while I attempted to eat the dinner that was getting cold. Given the opportunity to join us, he accepted. Immediately the sounds from his lips began to vibrate around the room. Stories were coming from his lips thick and fast, leaving me wondering if he was going to stop for breath. Half an hour into the continuous dialogue he said, "I just called in to see how you are." At that moment I burst out laughing which was just what I needed to break down the tension that was building up inside. I needed Danny's continuous talking, his rendition of the world outside, and his solution to every problem. So many fantastic, imaginary stories boom into my ear and I laughed till I could have burst. We had turned into a pair of laughing hyenas and I was doubled up with awful stomach cramp from Danny's lousy jokes. Anger, disappointment and depression had floated through the windows like a puff of smoke. Once again in a time of desperation Danny had come up trumps. His unannounced appearance began to create ripples in my head, with questions like, was he sent to calm down what could have become a volatile situation? The laughter laid my dangerous activity on the table for discussion to explore the funny side. The evening quickly passed into night and Danny's presence created a vacuum. I could not work out whether Danny had a specific subject he wanted to discuss. One thing was plain for everyone to see, his impromptu appearance mended a broken communication link, bringing us both back to square one, which made it tricky to tell Catherine that I was seeing images. So I decided not to show my appreciation again until I could do something without causing any major accidents. I was very glad to see the end of that day.

Bedtime was fast approaching; Catherine sat in silence watching television while I listened with the cat curled at my feet, occasionally sticking her claws into me, causing me to jump and shout, which set her crying from fright. Reflecting on the day's saga helped me to work out where I went wrong. Strangely, I could not find out how I could have done things differently, so I was stuck in an unresolved situation and my only option was to have a word with God. My faith was strong enough to allow me to talk or pray any time I wished. With no communication between Catherine and me, my thoughts entered another world where there was no darkness. Whether it was praying or meditating, I was at peace with God and his presence was pretty close. Our relationship was my main concern because the last thing I wanted was to upset Catherine in any way. What seemed like a few minutes concentration became hours. So much so, that she thought I was sleeping. Thank God it was time for bed where I could lock away any visual expression of pretence. Furthermore the date for the operation was on my mind, and I was hoping for a good result so I could get back to some kind of normality.

I lay in bed while Catherine decided to stay up late. The images I enjoyed were no longer there. I was in complete darkness. Still I convinced myself that it was just a blip and the light and the images would return the following morning, but somehow I could not get settled. The clot meant any sudden change in my condition could be irreversible, and that was my main concern. Catherine's late arrival in bed did not make the situation any easier, though I was pleased. Her warmth brought some comforting stability to my anxious thoughts. A few hours' sleep left me in good spirits and it was great to hear the birds singing their praises in readiness for the journey to their feeding grounds. The cat was scratching on the door to be let out and I wa hoping against all odds that the images would come back. Now, strangely my eyes were wide open looking for light, but my brain failed to alert the rest of me that something was wrong, for the images were nowhere to be seen.

Feeling distraught I started to blame my wife for her unprovoked attack to my good intentions. I could not get it out of my head that her behaviour created the setback I was experiencing. With all that erupting in my head I could not breathe a word to her in case I made delicate atmosphere worse. I went off to the bathroom to wash and know I felt my way to the living room, to sit and wait until breakfast was ready. Soon there was a knock on the door; it was Andrea and the lovely Angeleque the little girl who never failed to dispel any doubts I was harboring. From the moment she opened mouth to say "Hello Grancha." she would be doing something to me or with me, and one day I shall rename her "My Little Tonic."

Andrea had a special duty; she bathed my eyes and applied the eye drops. Angeleque, in the meantime amused me in all sorts of ways. But that day was special, because those girls' shared breakfast with me, and took away the fear of that disruptive night. Angeleque and I played her games, even though I could not see her beautifully turned up nose and captivating smiles. Andrea was ready to leave, but my tonic wasn't, she wasn't finished doing all the things that would make me better. Gentle persuasion was needed before she would concede that she was ready. Her actions turned smiles into laughter. Angelique was the source of my happiness, but that was not the whole truth. We hugged and kissed goodbye and then I scurried into the bathroom to have a good look in the mirror, trying to determine how much sight I had. Bear in mind only a few minutes before I could not see my granddaughter's face. I can't remember which came first, whether it was seeing my face, or praying, but what I was sure of was that I was praying so loud Catherine could have heard me if she had been standing outside the door. For a moment it felt as if I had fallen asleep, and I had awoke hearing my voice saying 'thank you God, for granting my wishes.' It confirmed that having faith was very important. What seemed to be the simplest of things to go wrong without good reason, nevertheless was put right. Only faith could have helped to overcome my anxiety created through the loss of sight. Overwhelmed with the latest development my spirit rose to an all-time high – to put it mildly – I was on cloud nine, as the saying goes. I walked back and forward to the living-room while the cat darted around my feet trying to trip me up.

I went to the kitchen to test the shapes I saw and make sure I wasn't dreaming. Buzzing with excitement and anticipation, I wondered whether to tell Catherine or not, it became one of my greatest challenges. She watched me maneuvering about, not knowing what on earth was up, and insisted I sit down. She was sure I was developing a metal disorder, and so she reassured me that everything would be done to make me better, and that she would always be there for me. Of course I was glad to hear her say that, and glad to here the difference in her mood from the previous night. Aware that I could loose the images again, I found in difficult to bring myself to reveal the truth. How could I explain that day I had seen shapes and a day later there was nothing? Now they were back. That would be too confusing for her, so I stuck to my decision. I didn't tell her but I did convince her I was happy. She had to go to her mother, so she kissed me on the cheek, and left me with the cat for company. The door closed with a bang; the cat was startled and she curled up closer to me. Automatically I looked down at her as she tried to climb into my lap. Surprisingly, I saw the cat as a ball of gray wool but I didn't know which way to hold her, till I felt sharp stretching claws on my legs. We were alone and I could not speak to answer back or to tell on me, so I began an enormous account of my experiences and what I wanted for the future.

It was so good to talk with no one to judge; I took time to air my guilty feelings and get them out of my system. The relaxed atmosphere made the time go quickly. It was the middle of winter and darkness still came early in the evenings. Deep in conversation with the cat, with my eyes closed most of the time it was impossible to notice the changes, until the landscape was in total darkness. I opened my eyes and became frightened. "Oh my God," I said. "What are you doing to me?" One moment I have vision, the next darkness. For a while it was utter chaos. I could not see the clock to know the time. The cat became nervous from my hysterical behaviour and jumped from my hands to go outside. There was not a lot I could do to defend myself, so out of fear I began to shake, if a knock had come on the door, I could not have seen who it was. What if someone tried to break into the house and bumped into me? It would cause more injury than I already have. Catherine might not be back for a long time yet. I started to panic. The adrenaline began to flow, giving me the courage to get out of the chair. I struggled to the doorway, found the light switch and turned it on. Not that it was going to help me to see, but it might deter the would-be burglar. I continued into the kitchen and switched on those lights as well. It wasn't until I got there that I realized I did not have any vision. I must have been walking with my eyes closed as I did not notice that there was light as I left the sitting room. I could not help but burst into laughter at how paranoid I had become. A cold breeze blew across my face, which indicated the door was open. I moved toward the door and closed it to feel the cat whiz across my feet, as she hurried in before being shut out. With the doors closed, the house was secure, so I sat down feeling more easily relaxed than before. The effect of those disturbing hours begins to unfold along with the fear and nerves that I needed to control. For weeks I have been telling myself, that I will accept my fate whatever it is, but after those few moments experience, I was sure that I didn't mean that entirely. I lacked the courage to accept without question what was happening to me.

The cat cried and danced around my feet as if she wanted to tell me something. She realized I wasn't taking too much notice so she wandered off to the front door to sat and wait with the occasional cry. To my surprise Catherine was on her way home and in fact she had already entered the gate. The keys made a noise as they opened the door. I praised the cat for telling me, because her presence brought relief from the pressure of being on my own.

As I could only see images it was impossible to tell the expression on Catherine's face when she walked through the door, but from the sound of her voice I got the feeling that she suspected something wasn't quite right. Feeling content, I began to smile, and her immediate response was to ask "Why are you smiling, with all the lights switched on?" Sitting in the dark never bothered you before, so why the sudden change? Guilty feelings clouded my thoughts. Worse, I could not give her a straight answer, so I mumbled, "I'm okay." To stop her asking further questions I redirected the conversation and asked her to tell me the time. She confirmed the time, which made it late evening. To suppress any inquiry into my experience, I inquired about my mother-in-law, "How was she and were there were any improvements to her condition?" I added, "What's the weather like outside?"

I wanted to tell her or someone about the development so badly. While the burden of deception shadowed me because I did not believe in living a lie. I sat quietly at the dinner table and avoided facial contact in case I exhibited a betraying expression. Supper was ready, and on the table, with the food cut into small pieces, and Catherine placed the spoon into my hand and positioned the dish in front of me. Things were going great, we ate our supper and I made the usual mess with minimum communication across the table. All the time I felt sure that she suspected something wasn't quite right. So I quickly ate and felt my way to the sitting room, where the television was already on. I sat and listened to the words while my imagination worked out the scene.

A few hours later Catherine joined in the usual evening ritual of 'square eyes'. It was the time of day when we would get the chance to sit down on our own and talk. The only good thing that came out of that evening's togetherness, were the sounds of the television. I was suffering with guilt and she curious about what happened during the day. Our stand-off game was in full action, so I listened to the sounds of the television until it was time for bed. As the hours went by and with very little to say I grew tired, so I made my way up the stairs to the bathroom where I prepared myself for bed. Soon I was tucked up in bed, while Catherine stayed up until the early hours of the morning, after watching all the films that were showing. It was her regular practice, which annoyed me greatly. Her preference for the late night seminars disrupted my sleeping pattern, which sometimes created frustration and tiredness. With the lack of sleep, the daybreak brought setbacks leaving me somewhat moody. It would be the times when a tapping noise vibrated the door. I knew it was the cat, she was awake and ready to get out. Her paws were the knockers along with her mewing cry. That morning the taps and scratches came on the door, and although I could not see, I made my way down the stairs and opened the door, and the cat with her usual graceful gesture, ran out.

My stomach rumbled for a cup of tea and it was pointless going back to bed. Time to put Mr. Hunt's teaching into practice, so I thought 'To hell with it,' if I get caught, so be it. I went to the kitchen counter to get hold of the kettle and filled it with water and set it to boil, in the hope of making a cup of tea without creating any disturbance.

The cups hung on hooks very close to each other, so with one slip there would be hell to play with noise. That meant slow and careful handling was absolutely vital. I had to remove one cup without knocking them against each other, and without allowing it to fall through my fingers to crash to the floor. I began the task of slowly removing the cup, gently feeling the shapes, and making sure that it did not collide or fall. Noise would bring Catherine down the stairs for another outburst like that she demonstrated a few days ago. I went through a sequence of operations with a minimum of noise and ended up with a wonderfully tasting cup of tea. Next I made the toast, which was much easier. I thoroughly enjoyed my determined attitude. That was my breakfast, which I had made myself, the feelings of independence almost made me think for a moment that my vision was back. But no, the possibility of making a meal without worrying about anyone excited me beyond words. If only that cat could speak, we would have a ball. Breakfast was over and I had made a big impact on my ego. The things I used were put back the way they were, or Catherine would have been sure to know I was up to something. The cup and cutlery were cleaned and put back into their right places without breaking anything. With precision everything was cleaned and back in their rightful places. I was on such a high, even though it was too early to be up. The vibrating sounds of snoring floated down the stairs giving me a ready-made excuse not to return. The alternative was to enjoy the tranquility of the sitting room. It was a very comfortable and relaxing place with its wide screen television, the latest model in stereo music systems, a luxurious dark red- and-pastel three piece-suite with matching foot-stool and a wall cabinet. The walls were lovingly decorated in floral pastel colours, with broad stripes flowing along the top and middle. The beautiful family portraits hung there, capturing the warmth and friendly atmosphere of the room.

Since the incident I had spent most of my time in that room, so it was important to have the best in music, which acts as therapy and helps to pass the time. Benji was instrumental in purchasing that system with a cracking headphone set with long flexes. A most exhilarating effort. The sales engineer gave us a training program, which with Benji's help I quickly mastered. How wonderful it was to have that kind of entertainment at my fingertips. Switch on and hey, presto! music was in my ears without disturbing anyone. A marvelous investment.

Feet up, eyes closed, I was transported into a world of absolute beauty, where everyone and everything floated carefree and peaceful as the music played softly and smoothly, subduing mind and body. How long I was there I don't know; but I was left feeling better than I could have wish. It was possible that I could have fallen asleep during those moments of ecstasy, which was what I needed to put my mind at ease. I was awakened by Catherine, who like a broken record, was asking what I was doing. I lifted up my head and thought, 'Give me strength oh Lord, before I say the wrong thing.' The rest of the day was the same. She was in a consolatory mood. Life became more tolerable as I pursued the true meaning of tolerance and patience.

Days before the next hospital appointment, Catherine returned to her mood swings as she judged her time between both her mother and me. Benji called round. He took me out to discover the changes that were shadowing me, but I was determined not to tell anyone in case the relapse became permanent, even though the images did not seem to be getting any better or worse. I kept an optimistic view with Benji, which kept him from being too far removed from the truth. Our trips gave me more hope, especially the occasional bumping into friends, whom I have not seen for some time and who hadn't been aware of my unfortunate mishap. It was a joy listening to their achievements both in family life and in the workplace.

Andrea and Angelique's visits became less frequent, which was a pity because the days of their visits brought out the best in me. She loved to play with the cat but the cat was afraid of her, so her arrival sent the poor cat running for dear life. Angelique was always too rough for the cat, but the cat wasn't too friendly towards children, no matter who they were. Angeleque always had so much to tell me that there was never enough time to complete it, so she was always saving something for the following visit.

As much as Andrea loved to come to see me, travelling with my little beauty every day for eight miles each way took its toll. I graciously accepted the fact she could not continue the travelling as much she been doing.

The day for my operation was near and my stomach began to turn into knots. Continually I talked or even thought about what the result might be, and how I wanted to behave during it. I knew enough about life to realize that things would never work as we hoped. But fantasy helped me to cope with reality.

Catherine packed everything I needed in readiness for the day. My youngest son Gary and his wife Lesley, drove me to the hospital. Unlike my eldest son Carl, Gary had never been to that hospital or in the area of the City before. But with advice from his brother and maps on hand, he was all set to go. All the plans were put into action. Gary rose to the challenge and so began our journey to the City hospital. Once again I was burdened with the saddle of worries, being unable to give directions through the City.

It was early March, the weather unsettled with rain and fog, did not make it an ideal time of year for travelling. We set off in the early morning to avoid the heavy volume of traffic that was usual for that time of the day. But we finally got there. My hopes were hinged on having the result I was desperately waiting for: the return of my sight.

The motorway was very kind to us, we cruised along easily. A small amount of light was getting into my eye, but the car was moving very quickly, so I was unable to focus on anyone or anything for long, and everything was blurred without shape.

The music on the car radio was loud and most of it was new, and everyone was chatty which made listening very interesting. I did not have to ask where I was, because Gary and Lesley readily volunteered the information as they navigated their way around the city.

They informed me of their position and from experience I could tell them with confidence what turn to take next. The ride was smooth and not stressful, even though fear was running amok in my mind. But, I was in control. Amid the hurrying drivers who play daring games to the detriment to other road users, weaving in and out like a dodgem car on the circus ground gave Gary moments of anxiety. He wasn't going to copy them, so he put all his energy into getting us there on time and safely. Gary, a banner-racing-car driver, his sporting hobby, was experienced in that type of driving behaviour on the racetrack, so he was quite comfortable with game the city drivers played. In spite of it all we arrived at the hospital on time, to face my fears.

Once again it was a repeat performance with one change. I was looking forward to the pending operation. Everything was progressing like clockwork, covering the journey for the second time; we arrived to the desk and registered my attendance, then sat and waited for the doctor to call. In a short time he called my name and I was nervous as a kitten, ready to curl up and die. After a quick examination, like all the others, the doctor confirmed that the operation would take place within the next few days. Strange yet exciting feelings obscured my mind with an optimistic view that I might recover some sight, if not immediately, certainly in the near future. The specialist's forecast went through the family like a bolt of lightning prompting them to overwhelming gestures of strength and concern as their grip tightened against my arms. The cheerful specialist lifted my spirit, which enhanced the good feeling I had. The specialist made another quick check to make sure there were no changes to his diagnosis and the operation was still on track. I told him of the deceit I was engaged in and how guilty it made me feel keeping it from the loved ones. Reassuring he said, "Not to worry, we will soon put things right." While he put the finishing touches to the admission papers, I was taken to the ward, which was to be my home for the following four days. It was a busy place; people and their trolleys were rushing past while Catherine and Gary guided me to my destination. It was a very long walk. For a moment my legs developed the shakes, as the hospital smells became more and more over-powering.

# Chapter 4

# DISAPPOINTMENTS

We arrived on the ward and surprisingly the nurse was waiting for me. She introduced herself as Mary and I was to be her patient during my stay in hospital. That gave me an air of satisfaction because I was given a name I could identify if in needed one, and that was comforting. She filled in a few forms before taking me to the bed I was going to occupy for the next three days. In no time at all I was settled in bed while she continued to show the rest of the amenities to the family. At last they had the chance to sit down with no problems from the road, other drivers or the pressure to be on time. We could relax and take in the atmosphere, while they told me the layout of the place: how many beds, where the amenities were, and other necessary information. I was given as much information as possible about their positions, as well as their rules and responsibilities.

It was getting late for the drive back, so hugs, kisses and good-byes were in order. I was certainly going to miss them, but I had plenty of time to prepare for that day. They went, and in an instant the realization dawned: this was a hospital ward with different conversational sounds and smells, which reminded me that I was away from home. Everything was alien and I had to deal with it. The hair on the back of my neck stood up and a lump formed in the back of my throat forcing tears to my eyes.

Although it was the day I had been waiting for, now that it had come my feelings were completely different from what I had expected. Mesmerized by the strange surroundings, I lost my grasp on positive thinking. I could not jolly well call one of the nurses to come and listen to my winging and self-pity, furthermore I was a grown man who did not believe in crying tears for something no-one could cure. I restrained my silly attitude and put to rest any sign of the weakness that was devouring my thoughts. From the sounds of the nurses' busy feet and clanging instruments as they carried out their duties, I put together a mental image and created a mental map of the ward, placing the beds, lockers, chairs and tables in the positions they had told me. I had a pretty good idea of sizes and space. My bed was very close to the nurses' station, which was situated opposite the main entrance, between the male and female wards and the corridor to the examination rooms. It was basically a short stay ward. There was a rapid turnover of patients, making the place busy and at times noisy. It was easy to tell the ones that were as blind as I was. The sounds and vibrations they created from the dragging of their feet, hands that slid along the beds and tables feeling their way to and from the bathroom gave them away. Their courage gave me hope that I could be blind and still retain my independence.

The actions of those men taught me that blindness was a mere setback which carries its own compensation. Those patients proved all wasn't lost and I knew that I could do the same. Listening to those busy nurses attending to each person as an individual and not just one of many patients was uplifting. Their sense of humor was fantastic, the jokes they sometimes whispered from another patient eased the tension and set my mind at ease. I was being prepared for an operation the following day, which made the nurses busy for the remainder of that evening and night, carrying out various tests and checks, while attempting to keep me calm.

Strange how things can work out. Halfway through the late evening I was feeling low and needed a friend to talk to. Well there is no other way to describe what happened next, for as if by magic I was joined by a fellow who lived locally. He heard my family and me talking, and from our accent he realized we were from one of the most beautiful parts of the country: Wales. His friend lived there, so he was delighted at the strange yet wonderful coincidence and introduced himself as 'Lloyd', sitting on the bed to become my friend who destroyed all thoughts of loneliness.

We talked and talked until the early hours of the morning. The shape I saw of him helped me to decide on his physical appearance, which I figured him out to be about 5 feet 4 inches and weighing about 11 stone, and white in color. During our conversation he would occasionally direct my attention to a fellow, who apart from his blindness, was also suffering from mental depression and his behavior was much to smile about. Lloyd would whisper in my ear to say the fellow was constantly brushing down his bed because there were lots of crumbs falling on it. He spent most of his time brushing off imaginary crumbs from his bed. It made a lot of noise in the middle of the night, and no one welcomes that sort of behaviour. He would also get out of bed, removing the covers, and that summoned the nurses to come to his aid. They had the pleasure of remaking his bed, getting him back in it, settling him down and reassuring him that there weren't any more crumbs or ants left on the bed, so it was all right to try and get some sleep. One could have made a big joke about it all, but it would not have been funny to that unfortunate fellow. In a way I felt sorry for him even though I could not do anything for him. I was in a similar position. I would hear a patient scream out that he was missing and that would send the whole place into an uproar, with staff looking for that wandering fellow. There would be cheers and laughter on his return. He would then get a lecture from Sister and be put back to bed. But, most lights were switched off, making it almost impossible for anyone to keep a constant watch on him. So even through he could not see much, it was as if he had someone guiding him. I could never understand how he managed to get far without doing an injury to himself or others. It also amazed me how he knew when the coast was clear, so that he could get away unnoticed.

Midnight and the operation was scheduled for the following morning. The nurses insisted that I get some sleep. Full of anxiety from the various preparation stages, I could not sleep. Too many things were on my mind. I asked the nurse for a sleeping aid, which I thought would do the trick, but even that did not work as I had hoped. The strangeness of the place and its unusual atmosphere, together with the knowledge that the operation might not be successful kept me wide awake. Lloyd was the perfect tonic he stopped my thoughts from wandering, whilst sleep stayed away. Those amazing stories, if I hadn't been there to witness some of his tales, I couldn't have taken then seriously. Listening to the various sounds of painful groans and worrying coughs, my heart thumped and my eyes grew watery. I opened my thoughts and asked the Good Lord for some help, which I knew everyone should be doing. Not until the early hours of the morning, did I get some sleep and within minutes the nurses were waking me up! I was given a quick wash, nothing to eat or drink, a few tablets, and then was left 'to rest' as they elegantly put it.

Putting on a brave face was extremely difficult. The pain from nervous exhaustion began to raise its ugly head. My hands and feet lost the will to move, while the walls seem to be closing in on me. Self-pity took hold with all its might and clear reason went for a walk. I thought, if I die here there would not be a need for the operation and I would not have to cry. Lying on the bed with no body else around, I could still here voices, and what was bizarre, one voice was coming from my own lips. When I thought about giving up, one voice would say, "What about the hard work Danny's friend has done for you? How about the way he helped you to cope with your problems? Are you going to throw it all away? That is very selfish."

The specialist's assessment was encouraging, but how long would I have to wait before someone came to my aid? Now a call of nature, I needed to go to the bathroom and rather quickly. The voice kept on bugging me. I was on a merry-go round and could not get off. The buzzer, yes, this is it – press that button. Well I must have pressed it so hard and long the nurse thought an octopus was strangling me. She rushed me to the bathroom and helped me undress. Sighted people sometimes fail to understand that a simple task can become a difficult operation. For instant when a male person goes blind, for a short time he loses his sense of direction, which makes it difficult to have a straight aim and to prevent flooding. Taken back to my bed I find the porter and his trolley waiting for me, and those voices keep rambling in my mind. I thought the bathroom interval would stop them but they became stronger and more overpowering. In a state of confusion I hear an unusual-sounding vocal which sounds like a baby learning to talk. To my surprise it was the porter asking me how I was and telling me he had come to take me down to the operating theatre. Well this was it, and I could not see to run away. A nervous smile was my response to his rational behaviour and he slid me onto the waiting trolley. Heart pounding, mouth dry, I plucked up the courage to accept whatever the result might be and make my peace with the human race.

I was propped up on the trolley like an exhibit. As the trolley moves through the ward I heard a voice whisper in my ear. Thank God it was Nurse Mary saying, "Be strong everything will be okay!" It sounded distant and faint; I could not understand at first what she had said. The trolley wheels were moving along the smooth wooden floor creating a noise like rain drops on a zinc roof, and sending tingling waves throughout my body and with the sensation of a runaway train with nowhere to stop. It twisted and turned, following the corridor, making the journey seem endless. The fear of the operation was no longer on the front burner; it was the ride that was eating me up. Unable to make a judgement about where I was, determining my position became an issue. I could feel the presence of people as they passed, which assured my brain that I wasn't in any danger.

Now, during our journey the porter did not say much to me, but he was very busy talking to other people whom he passed. How I wished I could see even the shape of another human being. Even if it had been possible my eyes were covered all along. I was feeling drowsy when the maneuvering stopped. Someone held my hand and said something that sounded like I was hearing it from a deep sleep. Drowsy and nervous, my reactions were slow as the team once again reassured me and gave me an injection that allowed the medical miracles to proceed. I gently drifted into the land of Nod. Three hours later, I was back in the ward, in bed, with nurses fussing over me, while the pain from the operation began to blow my brain apart. That pain was so extreme, it would be difficult to describe it. I screamed for something to ease the pain and the nurse was quick off the mark, with medication that knocked me out in a flash.

It was late evening and I awoke to find myself lying on my chest with my face buried in a specially designed cage. If I could have seen myself it would have been a shocking sight. The cage formed a mattress and pillow with my face expose to the floor, facing the underside of the bed. What I needed was my dog to lick my wet nose!

That position was very restricting; there was no chance of touching a friend unless he sat under the bed, which was impossible. My head was bandaged as tight as a mummy's wrap. Luckily the nurses were very attentive; one would come to see me quite often with the occasional drink from a straw especially made for me. With a fair amount of medication in my body it wasn't difficult to fall into a deep sleep, which took me through the night.

I woke up early next morning to find myself in serious agony, and in desperate need of a bodily function. I had no choice but to scream for the nurse who quickly came to my rescue. But not before there was a 'wee' accident. I can smile about it now, but it wasn't funny at all then. Life among us poor mortals began to take on some meaning. While the staff changed shifts the place sounded like a cattle market, with trolleys banging with their equipment, the scream of telephones, the buzzer bleeping by some impatient 'patients'. Those nurses' discipline climbed a notch or two, allowing organisation to prevail. My wait for the doctor to arrive and reveal the results seemed eternal. I prayed for a success that morning, but the end of my world was flashing before me. If the doctor had got it wrong, I was about to lose all faith in the medical profession, even though I was compelled to accept the result. The nurses changed my position in readiness for the doctor to see me.

Listening to other patients as some slurped their cup of tea, I yearned for a drop of warm liquid to wet my throat. That would have reduced the foul taste and smell escaping from my mouth. I wanted to be sick but I couldn't, because the pain was excruciating when I coughed or moved my mouth. So I waited and endured the discomfort. I remembered thinking that the way I looked lying on that bed, not having seen anyone in that position, must have been funny. I tried to have a peek but the bandages were too tight; no chance. Anxiety was rampant; patience became a meaningless word. There were noises and commotion as the nurses changed the beds, the cleaning staff banged the sweeping brushes and cleaners against the bed-legs, and I heard the flapping of slippers by patients escorted to and from the bathroom. But none of that broke my intense concentration on the result of my surgery.

Breakfast was in full swing, the tea trolley with all its cups and saucers was clanging away as the nurse poured and serves the tea. Amid that entire brain-torturing situation no one came to turn me over. Not only was I getting frustrated, my back was becoming tired and painful. In the distance I heard a humming sound and the unmistakable military footsteps approaching the ward. My hour of truth was near and I was about to learn my fate. As the sound of his shoes hit the wooden floor my heart was like a balloon ready to burst, my breath shortened while the rhythm stopped at my bedside. They were steps of the specialist who was standing over me in what seemed to be an optimistic mood, offering me some comfort. His hands were touching my shoulder while the nurse put me in a more comfortable position. In a soft well-spoken voice he said, "How are you today?" As he spoke his firm but gentle fingers removed the bandages from my head, while the nurse held my hand in a comfortingly, as if something terrible was about to unfold. The unveiling seemed to be going on and on, it halted, I thought it was the end, only to discover there was another layer to go. Finally he reached the patch and there was a hesitation. I remember that slowness as if he were teasing. The patch was off and the moment of truth arrived. His voice said, "Can you see my fingers?"

There I was, trying to see his fingers but nothing happened. Anxiety built up and for a moment I thought my eyes were closed, or why else could I not see his fingers? The frustration and anticipation mounted, my hopes were shattered. The operation was over, my eyes were open, yet there was no vision. My world was falling apart. The road to a nervous break down drew near. For the first time I thought that God must have forgotten all those hours I spent praying to him. The specialist and the nurse were talking to me but I did not hear a word they were saying; my body was sitting on the chair but my thoughts were far away. The

Images I had on arrival at the hospital were no longer there, but it did not feel as though I was in complete darkness. So, what was I seeing? Nothing. My mind took comfort; the atmosphere was a thick reddish mist with what appears to be a light-beam circling the parameter. Was this the beginning or the end? Still I clutched to the notion that one day I would regain sight.

Disappointed, I was taken to the examination room where the specialist carried out an intense inspection. The drop he used along with the bright light increased the disillusion. He calmly explained why I was unable to see as promised, but nothing was registering. My mind was a blank. I can imagine that he and the team were as shocked and disappointed as I was. Dumbstruck, I did not ask the important questions like why, what went wrong, what are my chances second time round. The nurse guided me back to the bed while a distant voice spoke to me. She was doing her best to cheer me up but if I answered or made a sound I cannot recall. Yet these words, which I feel sure the nurse had said sounded hopeful: there will always be another time. She sat me down at the bedside to await a late breakfast. With all the pain and humiliation I endured over the preceding days, hoping to restore my independence and masculinity it had never dawned on me that self-pity would become the order of the day.

On the specialist's return, once again he placed his hand on my shoulder and in a sympathetic but upbeat tone, assured me that the next time would be better and most of all, I would not have to wait long for that opportunity. The humility he projected persuaded me to accept that a second operation would almost certainly guarantee success. My feeling softened and my attitude changed. I was convinced that the unfortunate delay was a mere blip. He helped me to accept his persuasive advice.

Stripped of my hopes and dreams, it was a welcome feeling when the nurse brought my breakfast of tea, toast and orange drink. I wasn't crazy for food, but being a diabetic I had to maintain a balanced diet. Afterwards, I sat propped up in the chair like a dummy in a special position for a few hours until the nurse decided I must resume another torturing stint of lying on my stomach. My head fitted into this cage like a toilet seat.

I was one hundred and fifty miles away from home, in a strange hospital, in strange surroundings, with no family or visitors to talk with. It was little wonder that depression thrived. I needed those absent loved ones to share the uncertainty and the hopes for the future. From mid-morning that until late that day I was in a world of fantasy, with self-pity limiting my communication. Although I felt sure someone was trying to help me remain part of humanity.

Lloyd my friend sat on the bed and began to ask what was my real problem. I told him about my disappointing morning. He said very little in reply; instead he was itching to fill me in with the goings on during my period of self-pity. As I answered his chatter, he stopped and slipped in a few questions which I did not mind answering. I explained that the operation did not go according to plan and I was left in the same position, even though the specialist assured me that there would be a second operation. It seemed that wasn't really what he wanted to hear; but my feelings were ninety-nine percent in favour of my sight returning. Anyway he soon changed the subject to the newcomers and asked who was the craziest patient on the ward. From what I heared it sounded very entertaining. Our chat became so relaxing and the depression slowly melted away.

Recovering from an unforgettable morning, my thoughts focused on my wife Catherine and the family. I wondered what was happening, and whether they know my fate, but most of all, I was thinking how much I was missing them. Even the pain from the bumps, bruises and burns were of more comfort than a hospital ward.

Dignity began to regain its grip, but it was suddenly cut short by a surprising appearance of the nurse. She said, "The specialist has orders, that you should not sit up for long. Sorry, I have to return you to that favorite position, face down." To make matters worse I hadn't been eating properly and there was enough wind in my stomach to fly a kite. Now, I was breathing the air that circulated beneath the bed, which was dreadful. It must have been awful for those standing over the bed.

Lloyd was a very good man and stayed regardless of the smell. He gave me a running commentary of the ward activities and a sample of his life story, all flowing like a mountain stream. Fascinating stuff I thought; especially his war days. From his explosive anxiety, I gathered that he needed someone to talk to, as much as I needed to hear his voice. Like he did not have any visitors. In his conversation, he kept referring to his daughter who found it difficult to visit. But his story was not as straightforward as it sounded. He was trying to cover up something, or he was making excuses for her failure to travel the five miles to the hospital. My God, I thought. What if he was living one hundred and fifty miles from the hospital, he would be left to rot.

With my head stuck facing the floor and alone in the hospital I was grateful for his company regardless of the awful behavior of my body. I plucked up the courage to tell him what was happening. In a typical veteran attitude he put his head close to mine and said, "I have eaten, drunk and slept in worse smells than yours." On that note I was his audience and about to experience the living history of his war days in the trenches as a boy. 'Furthermore', he went on, 'it's a bodily function for crying out loud. It can only be stopped if you are dead and you are not ready for that, are you?'

His talk brought relief to my embarrassment and stopped my body twisting like a contortionist. Time seemed endless and I asked Lloyd the time every five minutes. I knew I would not be in that position forever, so a close watch on the time was important. The pitch of his voice changed, making me think he was getting fed up. Saved by the tea trolley, it was time for the last cup before lights out, not that it was of any use to me.

Lloyd soon made a dash for his bedside, preparing for that last cuppa. I was left to work out how far the trolley was from my bed. Like him, I too needed a warm drink. My thoughts started to run riot, trying to work out how I was going to eat and drink the cup of tea my stomach was crying out for. There was a small hole through the bed – but I was lying on my stomach. It seemed impossible. Still I continued to wonder. Little did I realize, due to the illness, my sense of logic had taken a nosedive left me disoriented and incapable of working out the simplest of tasks. The nurse reached my bedside and my fears were enormous, with those burning questions lurking in my head. Before I could utter a word, she said "Okay young man, let's turn you over and get you out of bed so you can have something to eat before you go to sleep." Like sunshine through the window my face radiated smiles at the relief of hearing those words. She turned me over and helped me out of bed onto a chair. Once again propped up with pillows, with a wet flannel to clean my fingers in readiness for feeding.

Unknown to the nurses I had already mastered the art of feeding myself. Ready to administer their dutiful good will gestures, they were pleasantly and surprisingly shocked by my refusal. At first they must have thought I was an idiot. I explained those early days of blindness, when I was taught to feed myself and they marveled at my achievement. One of the other fellows began playing-up. I could not help but smile at his actions, though not at his illness. The thoughts rang through my mind, why the doctors couldn't give him a pill or two to calm him down. A few hours of that behaviour and our attention became focused on this patient who kept walking up and down the ward. The heels of his slipper flapping against the wooden floor and made an enormous racket as he paced the length of the ward. What was amusing about that fellow was that he would wander out through the door and into the ladies' ward, or downstairs, yet he could not see to feed himself!

Every so often one of the nurses came along to point-out the positions of my dishes and put spoons in my hand and sat me up nicely. She was about to move off, but then she turned and whispered, saying that every patient is suffering with a sight problem, so no one is better off than the other. I felt able to forget table manners and allowed my fingers to do the job they were created for without a care. I tucked into the meal like a starving animal and put aside any feelings that I was being watched. Well, as the saying goes, a hungry stomach has no conscience! It took a while to consume my meal, blocking out the noise and interference coming from the workings of the place. As my belly filled, my mind relaxed. The different sounds from the moans and groans brought a smile to my face.

I thought I was pretty good in recognizing sounds and languages. But during my stay I was well and truly foxed. A nurse spoke to me and I thought I could recognize whether the voice was that of a male or female. Somehow, I dropped a bloomer. I knew when the Irish nurse spoke as she visited my bedside more often and was responsible for my care. There were Jamaicans, English, Malaysians and Spanish nurses, male and female. For two days, I had been listening to that voice, which I thought was of a female. It wasn't until late one night just before we were tucked in for the night that my care nurse arrived. Feeling brave, and in a very soft and quiet voice, I asked her to confirm whether that nurse with the voice I could not place was Italian or Spanish. To my horror she said, "He is Spanish!" I could have died. It was shocking to hear; dumbstruck was more like it, knowing I had been putting him in a bracket simply because of the sound of his voice. I am sorry but it did not conform to my idea of a masculine tone. Apart from telling Catherine, I could not breathe a word to any other person, the shame I felt was more than I could comprehend. The moral of this story demonstrates that when a patient is undergoing hospital treatment, it is not unusual for such a person to become disorientated and to lose their confidence, and be unable to make an accurate judgement. It was time for us to be tucked up in bed and once again it was the same old story, face down for a second night. That position was unbearable. I couldn't move because of the pain in my back and the cramp in my legs which were crippling. Tired from the day's ordeal it wasn't long before I was off to sleep, and thanks to the medication in my body, I had a good night's rest. I have no memories of that night.

Morning dawned and I was over the moon, when the nurse arrived at the bedside to turn me over and give me a cup of tea. First I lifted the eye patch, hoping that I would prove everyone wrong, and see the surroundings. But I could not see any more than the previous day: nothing. Taken to the bathroom, where I was helped to make myself presentable. It was a nerve wracking experience to be undressed by a strange person in a strange environment. It did not help that I could not see who was helping me. Unpleasant as it was, I gritted my teeth and got on with what had to be done, while the nurse was so patient and polite, gently assisting as I fumbled to find what I searched for. Those nurses were marvelous. Working with us blind and vision impaired takes a special kind of person with an understanding of when and how to approach at sensitive moments. Once finished, I was taken back to my chair and made comfortable and left to wait for the doctor's arrival.

The hustle and bustle of the nurses and the many doctors visiting their patients made the place sound like a racetrack. With the clattering of shoes on the wooden floor, the scratching of the trolley wheels and the constant ringing of the telephone I wondered whether I was in a hospital ward or a railway station at the busiest time of the day.

I was in a daze zooming in and out of one train of thought to another, sometimes waking up to reality. My nervousness impaired my reason; I have not been listening to my faith or to the kind words of the nurses and friends. Instead self-pity had overtaken my thoughts and I was focused only on myself. The doctor arrived carrying out his tasks, knowing that there was nothing more that could be done at that particular time. Still, he was enthusiastic to me, but not with the same commanding enthusiasm that he showed the morning after the operation.

Happy with the thoughts of home coming that evening, I knew it was only a case of patiently waiting for him to be satisfied with my progress and the precautions against infections were firmly in place. A quick look and the all clear was given. Good news, even though my mind was running riot. Excited, yes, to be going home, but disappointed about an impending return to an experience I wasn't looking forward to. Unable to see, I listened to what was going on around me and as I listened, the stories that were flowing among sighted patients were amazing. Without care they would broadcast their private affairs across the ward, as if they were the only ones hearing it. That took me back from a state of despair and made me take note of myself. The faith I had proudly endorsed had slipped and left me dangling. While those men told real life stories, some of which I could identify with, and others which were worse than I have experienced. Those stories compelled me to stop encouraging those foolish thoughts that drove me round the twist.

Lloyd, my friend joined in the exchanges, knowing that some of us were under the weather, so to speak, spiced up the conversation and turned it into a job of bringing out the smiles we were guarding against. One story sticks in my mind with passion. During the war the strongest helped the weakest. A mate had his leg blown off, and another was blinded from the blast with two others badly wounded, but who could walk. What was sad about it, they were miles away from safety and they had to carry the legless mate. The blind men carried the hammock with the legless mate, the two sighted, but wounded lead, guiding the blind men by rope while the other kept the rear. It was a moving story that made me feel stupid and selfish. I had all the comfort that was possible, yet I was not satisfied still feeling as if I was given the worst deal going. Lloyd could never comprehend the enormity of his help, in restoring my sanity during those trying days. But I could never forget him and thank him enough.

The ward soon became a hive of activity and in the middle of it, I could hear those distinctive footsteps moving down the corridor towards us, which I was ninety-nine percent sure were those of my man the specialist. He approaches the bed in a happy vibrant manner and asks how I was feeling! Oh God, I thought, should I tell him the truth or lie to him? I kept to the safe route. "Bearing up", I said. "Jolly good, Jolly good" he answered. He removed the bandages and looked into my eyes asking, "Can you see my finger?" I could not. "Well let's go", he said. He caught hold of my arm and led me to the examination room, where there were other doctors seeing to patients, probably with the same kind of result as mine. That time I went without nerves, after all I already know my fate. I needed to know when the new appointment would be. We entered and I sat down while her repeated the same performance as the previous day. Sore and tender from the lights, I was glad when he stopped. What followed was a very fruitful conversation of what he would do next time, with conviction and certainty about the result. I thought that his talk was patronizing because I had heard it all before, and from him. He was the expert, so gracefully I accepted his words and was grateful for his effort. I agreed to a second operation, which hopefully would change things for the better. Although I was disappointed, the chats we have renewed my courage tremendously. A nurse escorted me from the room who I asked to tell me the layout of the surroundings. She gave me graphic detail telling me what she could.

I walked beside her down the walkway which led into the female ward joining the corridor, and passed the nurses' station as we went onto the ward and my bed. Still I was stumped. I could not work out a picture of the place in my head, neither could I tell my left from my right, everything was so mixed-up. My happiest moment came when she put my hand on the chair and said "You can sit now." I had to phone Catherine and tell her that I was ready to come home. My heart was heavy as I meditated on the journey home and what life was going to be like until the next appointment. Soon Lloyd was sitting on the bed spinning some more yarns, some true, some slightly exaggerated, but he gave some relaxation with a few laughs, which I desperately needed while waiting to be taken home.

The call was sent to Catherine. Gary and Lesley set off and within four hours they were there to collect me. The journey was so relaxing I slept almost all the way home. I was a happy man. I was home, in friendly surroundings among the family, in a place where I could do most things for myself.

# Chapter 5

## THE LONG WAITS

It was great to be back home and to enjoy the comfort I had taken for granted so often. I appreciated my privacy, which strange as it may sound, had become very important in a hospital ward, mostly when I had to stand there not knowing who might be watching while I relieved myself. The nurses were very attentive, but they were busy people, seeing to other patients, some in a worse condition than I was. During such times I felt pleased that I was unable to notice anyone watching.

Settling down in my favorite chair to the delightful warm caressing feelings of the family's love, the disappointment of not being able to see began to fade. The cat rubbed her head against my legs, and cried to remind me she was there. I scratched her tummy in response to her, reassuring her that all was not lost. Bending forward giving her a good tickle rekindled the pleasure I'd missed. She rolled from one side to the other, lifting her tail, her paws gripped deep into the carpet pulling out bits of wool and creating a flurry. Once again she helped me to unwind, and to find my own space.

Catherine was busy in the kitchen preparing tea. She rushed before darkness fell so she could see her mother, Grace, who still needed her care and help. Although Catherine did not have far to walk, large trees along the roadside obscured the street lights creating blind spots and shadowed the street. This was an area which children used as a meeting place. It was a lonely, dark and secluded place for the gathering gangs. It was also very intimidating for a woman on her own to pass those marauding youngsters. Those children could be very quiet when making their plans of attack. This could be frightening for an individual if they were suddenly confronted with burst of laughter in a dark area. Yes, I was fearful for her safety. Tea was finally finished, which wasn't one of her usual meat and five veggies, more of a quick snack with a little more class. Eggs, bacon, tomatoes, beans and chips, served with a knife and fork and a beautiful white-lace tablecloth covering the dinner table. The meal was well received and thoroughly enjoyed. She quickly washed the dishes and set off to see Grace. Even though she had told Grace that her return could be too late for a visit – that did not deter her. Like most daughters she was close to her mother and it would be a cardinal sin if she did not go and make sure Grace was okay.

I was used to being left on my own but no sooner had she gone than she was back, which was surprising. After all it wasn't unusual for her to stay with Grace for long periods. Still I was happy to have her back; it was more than just the cat for company. She walked in the room where the cat and I spent most of our time; she slept while I listened to the conversations on the television, trying to build up pictures of what they were talking about. Sometimes I got it right, other times totally wrong, which could be demoralising. Catherine said, "Grace was happy to see me. So I told her what happened." She said, "There is hope for you yet." Grace is eighty-five years of age and she was quite capable of staying up most of the night worrying about us.

After a few nights of sleeping in a hospital bed where the environment doesn't allow the same comfort, that night I was looking forward to my own bed. Sitting in my favorite armchair with the warm comforting cushions wrapping my body like giant pair of gloves, my brain finds it harder to keep up with the programs. Catherine returns to the sitting room after a long relaxing soak in the bath and settles down to her favorite programs. By then, I must have drifted off to sleep, probably snoring too. Well it had been a long and tiring day; I retired to my bed. I bade Catherine goodnight and slowly felt my way up the stairs, where the bed in its full glory waited for me. Stress from the journey had caught up with me.

I went to the bathroom for a quick wash and brush and then to the place where the comfort of snoring, talking in my sleep, awaits me. "My bed". A welcome sight, or in my case, 'feel'. It was sheer ecstasy to be back in my own bed. I had no feeling of pain in my body and I still held onto the belief that one day I would recover vision. Gently I slid under the duvet and felt the cold cotton sheet against my skin. It was relaxing as an ice-cold glass of water on a hot dry sunny day. I paused to switch off the lights and test the images I have seen. No surprise, they stayed the same.

The pressure of the journey and disappointing results created a cloud of self-pity. I prayed intensely that God would help me gain enough sight to get around with minimum struggle. How long did I pray? I could not say because tiredness was in control and sleep was the cure.

When I woke the following morning, the Kochi bird was perched on the window-ledge singing songs of praise, while the cat was happy to have me home and cried to be let out. Thank goodness the images were still there, but with a difference. They seemed stronger, but not clear enough to identify my surroundings without the use of my memory. My hopes strengthen: perhaps the next operation would be successful. That was the nagging question. Would I be strong enough – mentally? Instead of lying in bed being a cynic, I took an optimistic view, got out, found my way to the bathroom and behaved like a sighted person. It was weird, I was determined to make a cup of tea before Catherine woke. I wandered down the stairs and headed for the kitchen where the joy of being home – meant I wasn't lonely. Thank goodness Catherine had not rearranged the furniture! The cat was becoming a nuisance at my feet, making me nervous, but hey, that's unfortunate. She could not realise her actions put my life in danger. Anyway, I successfully made the cup of tea without smashing any of the wares, and better yet there had been no noises. I sat at the table drinking what to me was the most wonderful cup of tea – one I had made myself.

I had to realize that I had been through a traumatic experience, being away from home and in hospital. I was disoriented, while trying to navigate my way around, and I was tiring, but it took time for my brain to memorize the layout. I made my way back to the sitting room where I had my first fright hearing scratching sounds at the back door. What could it be? Oh my God, if it a burglar I could not identify the sound. Bravely, or stupidly more likely, I turned and looked, an automatic reaction. The cry was loud and clear, it was my trusted friend the cat. "Thank God for that!" I said, and she darted in while I returned to the sitting room.

The sudden fright brought back dreaded memories of the meal I cooked, which upset Catherine because I'd put our lives in danger. All because I was desperate to please her and at the same time to regain some independence. The door incident could have been far different. It highlighted the dangers that were beyond my control: a change of strategy was essential to my safety, especially noises coming from doors or windows.

Curled up in the chair, feeling sorry for myself, the clock struck ten, signaling the time Catherine usually got up. She adored clocks of any description; quiet or noisy, to her each one had a special characteristic that deserves a place in her home. That particular clock was her favorite and it would strike on the hour, quarter and half-hour. Its chimes were very loud, and seemed to occur just at that moment when an interesting announcement came on the television. There where times when I felt like throwing it through the window, but I would have hated to imagine what Catherine would have done to me. Still, I had an ace card that would win me the game. An enormous amount of time on my own listening to the television wasn't giving me the comfort I needed to calm and stimulate my brain, so Benji and I went to purchase one of the latest stereo music systems and top of the range headphones. Benji loved and possessed all types of musical recordings. He spent hours recording some of that music onto tapes and during his visit he would add a tape to my collection. He was aware that I could not read labels, so he reorganised the record shelves, giving me a selection of records, CDs and tapes, all put in order of fast or slow with identifying markers between each section. That was an absolutely wonderful idea. I simply had to find the shelf marker and make my choice of music. Having selected the music, I slipped the headphones on, lay back, and dreamed. As the music hit my soul and transported me to another plane the odd sounds of Catherine's footsteps downstairs disturbed the rhythm, forcing my attention to my breakfast. I made my way to the kitchen to await my breakfast, but not a word was said, which I found strange, because she surely should have seen some sort of changes, like the sink wet or the warm kettle. I could not believe it, where there no clues of my misdemeanor? Whatever her reasons, I felt safe with her silence. She continued to make breakfast without speaking, so I returned to the sitting room. Crowned by the headphones listening to some of my favourite songs – I took my soul back to a world of beauty and pleasure. Seductive sounds caressed my eardrums and lifted my fantasy amongst the clouds, and there in my musical world I found peace. What seemed like a long time was in fact a few minutes, until I was disturbed by one of man's most loved inventions. Catherine said, "The telephone for you." All good things come to an end, as the saying goes, but this was the wrong time. Catherine also wants me to join her for breakfast as usual, so I do, the cat marching at my feet.

Like jungle drums, the word got around that I was home. The telephone rang until it was red-hot. Everyone wanted to know the same thing – could I see again? When I told them about my disappointment their voices dropped in sympathy. Having to repeat the procedure so many times made me pessimistic about my chances. From enjoying any music top those depressing calls, I'd lost my appetite for the boiled eggs and toast Catherine served for me.

Andrea and Angeleque arrived; the little girl with a thousand voices and the ability to extract answers in seconds, which had taken me years of growing-up to achieve. She was a busybody who never took 'No' for an answer. Her exuberant happiness infected my spirit with laughter and lifted my gloom. But there was more encouragement that day, too: Benji turned up and with that man I never knew what was going to happen next. He could be so funny, but he knew I wasn't at my best that day. So he came up with stories that stopped me feeling low. As it grew late Catherine had to make her usual visit to Grace. Benji heared that she was going and his jokes came thick and fast. Depression floated away like a cloud and life seemed more worth living.

Between him and Angeleque, I found the courage to walk and bump into the chair, table, or step on the cat's tail, which was a great cause for mirth. The only trouble was they left me before Catherine returned, and I sat alone in silence, alone in my darkness.

I have always been afraid of the dark. I never welcomed nightfall, but at that time, still reeling from the experiences and disappointment of the last twenty-four hours, I felt as though I was enveloped in threatening darkness. Waiting for Catherine's return I had only the cat for company and the tension from the previous day reached boiling point. Who could blame me for shouting? I needed help to regain my composure, to allow my pitiful brain to accept the five weeks' wait, which really wasn't a long time. After all I had already waited five months to see this specialist.

I fought to stay in control of my situation, but even so the simplest task become a major obstacle. My attitude towards those whom I loved was a topic for concern. Sounds awful? Of course it does. Reason and logic were abandoned as they always are when we are afraid. I tried telling myself, "Pull yourself together." But it didn't matter what I thought or what I did, the force of my fears had taken over and I couldn't stop it. Inside it a volcano raged, ready to obliterate everything I had worked for. It shamed me to recall my unworthy behaviour and I suffered much guilt. I have always conducted myself respectfully. I was becoming a pitiful sight. The anger that had built up inside created a tendency of mischief making. An unkind and derogatory manner was my mask to hide my anxiety – a cruel play, but I knew no-one would thump a blind man, no matter how nasty he might be. Wrong, yes I know it was. But that's the only way I was able to cope with the disappointment and the blindness. I could not see people's expressions and their body language. So I often misunderstood people, thinking that their good intentions were patronizing. So I had to invent something that would relieve the pressure. I invited anyone to explain how one should cope rationally after being subjected to sudden blindness. I am sure there are others like myself who have had similar experiences. I truly hope that one day these days fear will be addressed, and a logical conclusion reached, which would help others in the future, who like me suddenly go blind. Angelic, Benji and the cat played a dominant role during those five weeks; they switch their role-playing on and off to suit my temperament. That simple strategy made the days and weeks pass more quickly than I had anticipated.

# Chapter 6

## THE MUSICAL STEPS

Five weeks passed: and now my anxiety grew as I went to face another espisode at the hands of the specialist. This time there were changes in the arrangements for my transport. I had to rise early to catch a bus for the three-hour journey to the city and then face another hour and a half by taxi to get to the hospital. The long laborious journey occupied my mind, letting in mischievous and damaging thoughts. By the time I arrived at the hospital I had worked myself up into a frenzy. In my view everything that could go wrong had gone wrong. All I could think about were the previous results and a sense of foreboding filled me. I saw shapes around me, dim lights flashed by. Noises from doctors, nurses, and patients, or who else I could not tell. I cannot recall how long it took Catherine or the nurse to get a sensible response from me. It could have been seconds or minutes. It seemed like years.

Once again I was in hospital, in the same ward, with the same doctors and nurses and staff. But of course the patients were different, a passing parade of people which always included some unusual characters, allowing an opportunity for comedy. I went through the first day's preparation, check in, and register, blood tests, temperature and blood pressure, urine test, operation schedule time. And because I am a diabetic, a diet sheet too. Travelling since the early hours of the morning had left me feeling extremely hungry. Furthermore I was so terrified that the operation would go wrong and leave me blind, that my appetite for food was not great. My last meal was at ten p.m. that evening. It sounds so final. However, I was looking forward to it, as if it really was in fact my last meal. There was some good news: I was scheduled first patient for theatre. Oh God, I thought, if everything continues like this, the operation might just follow suit and be successful. There's more comfort. This time I have a visitor.

Catherine stayed in the City while the operation was being performed. It was a wonderful feeling waking up and having my wife at my bedside. She had been unable to visit during the first operation, which was very sad for both of us. Her decision to be close throughout my stay meant the world to me. Being the first patient to sample the surgeon's knife meant that I would recover during daylight hours. At least Catherine would not have to travel to her lodgings after dark. My hopes were dashed. Talk about things going wrong. During the operation, my blood pressure went up, delaying the recovery time. Catherine was in turmoil with worrying. Strangely, I had never suffered from this condition before, so the episode was puzzling. The long wait alarmed her. She said, "I thought something had gone seriously wrong!" She constantly asked the nurse for information, but no one could answer her fears. Even though I was a pitiful sight, my return to the ward was a source of tremendous relief. At least I was still alive.

Late evening, when I regained consciousness, I was wracked with an excruciating pain. Through the agony, I heard a voice saying "It's all right." I knew whose voice it was, but I could not see anything. Catherine reinforced her presence by holding my hand, while I tried to keep from screaming with pain. But, oh the comfort in knowing she was there! She was able to summon the nurse and tell her of my plight. She observed first-hand the horrible sleeping positions, face down, bum projected like a pyramid, and my grunting and groaning. A powerful sedative was administered, which knocked me out in a flash. I have no idea when Catherine left my bedside. It must have been late. I'd worried about her walking a strange city street after dark to return to her lodgings, but although she was nervous, she arrived there safely.

The new day dawned with me still wrapped and stuffed like an oven roast, facing the underside of the bed with my bum stuck up like a pyramid. I was breathing in a confined space, and stifled by the smell of my body odour. I had first to grin and bear it and to hope that there was nothing worse to come. The noise of shoes on the wooden floor, of schussing trolley wheels and rattling containers filled the air around me. One by one my senses started working, although my heart thumped like a jackhammer.

I searched for the call button, but it was nowhere to be found. What could I do? My water work was about to burst its bank, but even if someone heard my call, would they meet me under the bed, which was the direction, I was facing? I shuffled my feet in the hope that someone would see them. Not knowing what time of day it was, I listened for the sound of the specialist's distinctive footsteps, worried he might turn up while my bladder was bursting. My movements became more aggressive, as I desperately tried to get someone's attention. I was about to wet the bed when I heard that musical tune, "Hello Roy, I'll help you to turn over". I forgot about the footsteps and breathed with relief that help had come only just in time. But then once I was turned, I listened for those footsteps intently. I heard him approach as the heels of his shoes hit the wooden floor followed by the soles and toes, and his fitted steel caps created musical notes, almost as if the shoes' owner was practising a dance. Yes, it was "Mr. Cool the Specialist." But how much of a champion was he going to be to me?

While I waited for him, I asked the time every five minutes, only to be told again and again "Be patient." Finally, in the distance, amid the sounds of nurses, patients, trolleys and constant ringing telephones, the penetrating sound of those shoes filled the ward. My body shivered with joy, as if I was listening to the London Philharmonic at full stretch. He took a different route to my bed extending my anxious wait. But finally he was standing there, and quietly said, "How are you?" I was so flabbergasted that I cannot remember answering him. Bending or kneeling in front of me, I do not know which, he gently removed the bandage. Nervous and worked up for fear that the surgery had not worked I almost wet myself. At the same time questions began to bombard my brain; what if it did not work, could I have another operation? Or would I become totally blind? Those few moments were sheer hell while the bandages being removed. I prayed that I would see his face.

It took minutes, which seemed like a lifetime of torture. His cold fingers touched the skin of my forehead, signaling the end of the bandage. While a soft gentle voice whispered "This is it, your moment of truth." He removed the eye patch to reveal a thick substance that covered the eye. A cold soothing lotion was used to clean the eye and went trickling down my cheeks as my heart went into overdrive. All the solutions were cleared, one hand firmly held my head while the surgeon waved the fingers of the other. In a positive and reassuring tone he said, "Open your eye and tell me if you can see my fingers?" By then light had already penetrated the lid. I did what I was told and opened my eyes. Oh my God, the biggest, greatest of smiles was greeting me! The picture was wonderful. Everything in that ward came to life, with the fingers of my champion "Mr. Cool", playing the leading role.

My feelings were indescribable, but exciting. I saw the lights, which were pink in colour, and yes, I *did* see his fingers. Excited, elated, my emotions were running wild. A roller-coaster began and I wanted to shout and tell everyone that I could see again, albeit mistily. For the first time in eleven months I felt safe. I have regained some sight, not excellent, but enough to get me around obstacles. The nurse in attendance shared my happiness, which was greater than if I had won a fortune. There were lots of activities going on that morning, making the place buzz as if it were filled with an enthusiastic group of children at meal time. Mr. Cool and I realised it was a good result. Cool as ever, he took hold of my arm and guided me to the quiet of the examination room, where he continued his examination along with his colleagues.

I had been waiting that morning to hear the musical sounds of Mr. Cool's shoes hitting the wooden floor with precision. Gutted, I missed them because he took a different route. Now though, I was about to get the full orchestral rendition including brass. As he marched down the corridor holding my hand, the sounds from those shoes vibrated through my weak body sending my spirit floating like a trapeze in full flight. For a moment there was a feeling of absolute silence; my brain suddenly stopped giving commands and my hands and feet just floated along. What was ironic was that the specialist, 'my champion Mr. Cool,' was talking to me, but I did not hear a word he said. The images were misty, but I could walk out through the door on my own, or in time I could run a marathon. That burning desire to regain my independence was getting stronger. It was only a matter of time. Unfortunately, Catherine missed out on the exciting hour. If only she could have been there to record to the expression on everyone's faces the moment I uttered those words, "I can see the light." Like me the specialist was surprised, his body language and the echoing tunes from those shoes convinced me, the result is what he had hoped for.

Once again my case evoked a great deal of interest, and even in that examination room his colleagues took turns examining my eye, and to give their opinions in medical jargon, which was Latin to me. Busy people with lots of patients waiting, the discussion was cut short. Within four months I had two admissions, had been to hospital a total of seven days, but on my return journey from the examination, I saw the nurse for the first time. I could now put on a face to the name I had come to depend on. I moved my head like a windmill, hoping to see something that would match the images I had build up. The problem was that I could not identify anything or anyone, unless I was within inches of them. Looking around gave me the impression I was seeing through a glass-bowl of pink jelly-like liquid. What was more interesting, as my body moved the picture became wobbly. Although I was happy with the sight I had, I still couldn't find the bathroom on my own. As I was taken back to what I thought was the continuation of an embarrassing position in my bed I was pleasantly surprised. It was no longer necessary to lie on my stomach, with bum perched like a beacon under the sheets. I could now sleep more comfortably.

For two days I had been listening to the different voices of different characters. I'd tried to label each one as tall, short, fat or slim, black or white to paint a picture of them so the stories would make sense. But when I sat up in bed to survey the ward, I was hoping to see them and discover if my mental assessment was right. Sadly, I could see only the ones on either side of me; it was such a disappointment.

Still I was looking forward to Catherine's visit because I knew she would be fascinated with the latest development. She'd had to travel to many hospital appointments with me and she had seen a steady decline in my situation. But today, I felt privileged and humble, because something new and wonderful had suddenly happened. My head spun in excitement, and it was difficult to concentrate on any other sound except Catherine's voice. I yearned to hold her hand and to thank her for being there. Thoughts of gratitude were uppermost in my mind and I wanted to tell her how I was feeling. The unique fragrance of her perfume stimulated my emotions. As it got closer, my heart raced to give her the news. The wait for her to reach the bedside seemed like a lifetime. There were smiles, hugs and tears which turned into laughter, as we celebrated overwhelming feelings of joy. Although she did not share my optimism, I had no doubt that one-day I would I see every line on her beautiful face again. She warned me that it would take more than words to fulfil my wishes. But, I was convinced, though I needed the luck and prayers of Saints. The warm pleasantries were over but Catherine wanted to know why my vision was still poor? She went to ask the nurse.

Minutes later, she returned with the nurse to my bedside. The nurse explained what was done during the operation, and she confirmed that there were no guarantees. The good news was that I could go home that day, as soon as the medications were ready. Although I was unable to go on my own, the feeling I had was similar to the happiness I enjoyed at the birth of my first child. I was overcome with relief. She collected my belongings in readiness for my departure. At least the operation was over and I had conquered the fear of whether it would be successful the second time round.

I had prayed very hard for a good result, and in a funny way I knew it would be. The result wasn't excellent, but gave me time and left me feeling that my prayers would be answered. It was time to shake hands with my bedside friends who had kept in touch during Catherine's absence. It was also time to have a word with the nurses, even though it took a while to match voices to names. The fact was that I had been at a disadvantage from the time I was admitted to the ward; it was important to have a clear image of those wonderful people who had given me so much attention. Of course I was in a hurry to get home; all I wanted was to say thanks and then get away from the hospital. It wasn't because of ingratitude or dislike but rather because of tiredness from that dreadful sleeping position. I wanted a quiet place where I could sit or lie down, whatever the case may be, to reflect and be still, to listen to my voice and wrestle with my own thoughts, that's what I wanted. I had a burning desire to walk without a guide; I wanted to be home where I could make an early start.

It was already dinnertime and I wondered if someone had forgotten me. I was asking the time more often as my patience became frail. Someone must have heard my lament and the nurse appeared with the medications which were special drops. She escorted me to the examination room, bathed and dressed the eye, and explained the correct way to apply the drops. The problem was that if I tried to apply the drops I would poke myself in the eye each time. I could not see how close they were to the eye. Half an hour after the examination all I could see were reddish clouds, but I wanted to get home so badly I did not say a word about it to anyone. The discharge papers were ready. Catherine signed them for me. She also bought a box of chocolates for the nurses, to say 'thanks'. Suddenly the sixty-minute hour drastically shortend to fifty minutes as we race to reach the bus station. But there was one more hurdle to overcome, a short interview with the social worker.

Eleven months had gone by since I became blind and the cost of travelling to and from hospitals, doctors, and clinics and other places had been astronomical. Having been registered blind after the first operation, I was granted travelling expenses, which was a great help. The social worker wished us good luck and refunded the travelling expenses. I knew she was a female person but nothing more; I had not seen her face. It wasn't until six months afterwards that I met the lady again, and saw her face for the first time. We went to the reception where a taxi was ordered to take us to the bus station. We slipped and shoved our way through the city's endless traffic jams to the coach station. The mere sight of the coach was sheer joy because home was the next stop. At the coach station we sat and rewarded ourselves with a salad roll and a cup of tea while the bright red color in my eye slowly changed into a lighter shade. It was a well-deserved break, with just enough time to eat our food. While passengers queued to board the waiting bus, it was the first time that day we weren't hanging about waiting for someone, which was nice for a change. With no vision there was little chance of spotting excitable behaviour amongst travelers. There came an announcement over the speaker saying "Please do not feed the birds, they might dirty on your heads!" At last my dreams were slowly coming together; the coach began to move and the feeding birds in its path fled away leaving us to travel one hundred and forty nine miles, a-three-hour journey.

I had six-weeks to wait until my next appointment so I could relax, feel good, and be surer of myself. The good news made all the difference. The announcement of my stop echoed through the bus. The hair on my head began to dance with enthusiasm as though I was wearing a hive of bees for a cap. I'd had several setbacks after hospital visits, but I have never returned feeling so happy. The bus pulled in to the stop, but despite the joy leaping about inside I still had to follow Catherine's lead. She had not said much throughout the journey. She was thinking her thoughts, I suppose, "Thank God it's over!" We got into a waiting taxi and in a few minutes she was opening our front door. The rest of the evening was a repeat performance of all my many homecomings. But this time I was in an exultant state of mind. I reported my feelings and intentions to my trusted friend the cat who always mewed a musical tone and listened while he washed her face against my feet. It was difficult to understand her advice because she lacked the ability to utter words in English. Our little talk had to end. I'd gone through an exhausting few days of travelling and uncomfortable hospital incarceration. My bed was an exciting prospect. It would be a pleasure to lie on my back rather than that ridiculous position, facing the floor, as I did after the operation.

I'd had a hectic day, exposing a tender and sensitive eye to the sunlight and dust, so it was in my interest to rest. But the phone rang red-hot with calls from family and friends, all concerned, and all wanting to know if the operation was successful. Those acts of kindness made me feel special because people care. Frightened that I might trip over the cat making my way up the stairs, I paused and looked for her, but her colour blended in with the carpet which made her impossible to spot. I had to shout "Get out the way you daft thing!" in case she followed the sounds of footsteps shooting up the stairs like a rocket. Did the cat understand me? I thought perhaps she did.

I could not justify staying up late even though I was missing Catherine's company. My bed was calling me. The surroundings were free from squeaking trolley-wheels and wandering patients, and I smelled only the fresh clean sheets and the seductive aroma of Catherine's perfumes. I managed a trip to the bathroom guided by the banister rail to carry out the necessary functions. On my return to the bedroom, I could feel my furry friend curled up on the mat outside the door. Gently I brushed her tail and retired to the waiting bed.

Lying in bed hoping to get some sleep, I found that thoughts vital to my recovery suddenly erupted. My diabetic condition was in rapid decline, so instead of getting off to sleep my mind began to grapple with goals I wished to achieve. The medication had to change because I needed stronger and more rigid control. But it was not be as straightforward as I anticipated because determination and will power would be vital. Regulation was the key to my success, in three ways: application, a rigorous testing program, and a good diet. My fingers would become like pin-cushions, my diet would be salad and more salad. I would be like a rabbit on two legs. Then the daily injections all over my body, and sooner or later I will become a giant chive, hoping that no one squeezes me. With the number of holes that I was about to insert into my flesh, the slightest squeeze would spring a leak! My biggest fear was that everything had to be done at set times. How would I cope disruptions? I worried, but eventually tiredness claimed even my troubled mind and I fell asleep.

The next morning I woke to find my brain buzzing with the same determined thoughts. I would take the all-or-nothing decisions and set the restoration program in action. Some members of the family thought I was asking too much too soon, but I was confident that if I handled things properly, there was a good chance I would regain my vision. My will-power was tested over the following weeks and months as the rough regimes of different treatments collided; the whole thing became extremely hard work.

The misty world, in which I lived, was a demoralising place for a once-independent man, who was constantly bargaining for help. It made me feel like a child and if the truth had to be known, my helpers sometimes emphasised my helplessness. The was a knock on the door which could have been anyone, but it was my friend Danny 'Mr. Know-it-all.' Well although I was glad to see what I could of him, his voice sent my depression up through the sky like a rocket. His voice and personality devoured the room and melted away the attention my cat needed, sending her scurrying for cover as confusion battered her eardrums. Danny was an extremely bitter medicine, which had to be taken in small doses, although in reality his help in my recovery was unquestionable. His communication was never subtle. His approach left listeners bemused. As he toyed with my patience, I knew that I could do nothing to curtail the mountain of information he poured out. I had been secretly inventing a special zip for his mouth. Admittedly some of the information was of value to my particular circumstance, but most was only hot air. Once he started there was no stopping him. Thank goodness his visits were short, but long enough to scatter the house-dwellers. So in a submissive way I was content to have Danny's presence because he brought programs of alternatives which are important to my plans.

My positive frame of mind paid off; it strengthened my outlook and made the pending medical appointment seem ordinary. Although it was to be a very important visit to determine how successful the operation had been, I also knew that improvements had gradually taken place. Six weeks quickly passed and once again I was in submission to my Champ, "Mr. Cool", the firm yet charming man who captured my soul with those musical steps. The examination room was much lighter than I had imagined. Through the mist I saw the layout, with each item looking as if they had been joined together. I sat down and the examination began with a couple of drops to relax the eye muscle. Soon I heard these famous words "Jolly good. No deterioration. The healing process has begun so it's just a matter of time." Funny, I thought, luck never entered into his thinking. He was confident in his skills and abilities. My legs shook and my body sought relief. I wanted to shake the life out of his hands, but that would not help the next patient. And furthermore the drops obscured what vision I had. He prescribed a reduction in the number of drops, reinforcing my confidence in my improvement. Excitement overwhelmed every fiber of my being. If Catherine had been present I would have given her the biggest kiss she had ever had. There was hope for me yet. The biggest decision was about to be made for my future. "Registration of my vision." No doubt about it! I was officially blind as of that day. My fate was sealed and there was nothing anyone could do about it. How I yearned for sight, at least enough to get me about with some degree of independence. That was a gut-wrenching decision to accept. But I had known all along that I was on borrowed time. It could have happened at any time during a fulfilling lifestyle. My only chance was a miraculous one.

Sight. For the first time since that operation had taken place, a bout of depression entered my thoughts. Catherine's face might add a memory to my collection, bringing pain to my already weak frame of mind. Leaving hospital I somehow had a renewed surge of strength. Determination and control were the key. Diabetes' greatest challenge if there were to be any chance in getting some sight. I promised myself that my diabetic condition would never be the controlling factor of my life. I set myself the challenge that enabled me to write this story.

# Chapter 7

## THE CHALLENGE

After a few days at home, family and friends began to suggest hobbies or interests within the community to stimulate my brain, in the hope of getting me back into some kind of activity. They thought I needed something to occupy my mind, taking me out of the house and placing me into the community and among others.

A volunteer member from a community project regularly called to see how I was. We would talk about his work and what was involved. His visits heralded an intense introduction to join their group. Even though my vision was poor and I could not read or find my way around, he insisted that wasn't a problem. If I joined he said, "You will be collected, taken back home and read to," which was excellent. At last there was something worthwhile to get my teeth into that could benefit the community. Having worked within the community for a number of years, I had won much respect, which was an asset to the group. This respect was more important to the group than the ability to see.

I had taken great interest in giving and receiving respect. Yet with all my knowledge of my community, I had failed to appreciate the beauty of its natural surroundings. I was always too busy to appreciate the changes that were taking place, as the miracle of nature collided with human endeavors. Walking along the street with my friend Benji, I was overwhelmed with the constant recognition I enjoyed from young and old alike. My reception helped to reinforce my determination to bring some sort of improvement to the neighbourhood. Catherine became more relaxed because I was getting out, and my thoughts were occupied with a subject that was far removed from just my vision.

Benji was still on my case. He would not allow me to go anywhere until he had checked it out and he was sure that my disability wasn't taken for granted. The protective attitudes of Benji,

Andrea and young Angeleque left me with feelings of guilt. I was aware that they had lives of their own and needed some time for themselves. So I was very happy to join the group. After one year in darkness fighting boredom, worrying about what shape my future would take, joining the group was part of the independence I desperately sought. The information that was given at my first meeting was amazing. They told me what my rights were and what was available for my condition. Where had these services been when I needed them? They always came into action far too late; never when I was at my lowest and in desperate need of help. Luckily for me I enjoyed excellent support from friends, but more importantly I accepted my situation and took a positive view in order to make best use of my misfortune. To be a significant contributor to this community group, I had to reject any thoughts of getting back into work, which would have been a dream. There was a lot of time to focus on that subject. If by some intervention I should regain my heart's desire to work, that would be a bonus.

The successful business I had built up over the years was crumbling, and there was very little I could do to save it. Despair took away the positive attitude that had been there on the inside. The importance of maintaining peace of mind was a key factor in preserving my sanity. Determined that I would continue to adopt new ways of tackling obstacles and of approaching people. Establishing some kind of normality to my lifestyle I had to overcome my situation. A journey of adventure was my everyday feeling; my aim was to achieve the group's objectives. Yes, disabilities had put an end to my working life. However it made me realise there was more to life than work. Even though I have always harbored a Christian faith I never had allowed it to flow as it should, which would have helped me to understand that possessions without health were no good. During my retirement years, I thought, would be the right time to devote energy to my faith. It was easier to keep it private and personal, while I carried out my get-rich policy.

Those thoughts, those sets of rules worked fine until I was fifty-five. I wasn't quite ready to retire, but the plug was pulled, plunging me into the world of darkness. During that time I had been living in the shadows of blindness. During my early years as a young production-engineering apprentice, I knew I was in one the most dangerous trades to the eye. To contemplate doing otherwise would have been a travesty because that's all I ever wanted to do since I left school.

My parents believed in my quest and gave me the start I needed and with determination I rose to management status. It was a great achievement for a black immigrant boy with one eye, in a strange country. A position that lasted eleven of my eighteen years of service. The training from those days gave me the foundations for good leadership qualities. Now, I was blind, so the world was there for me to explore and to take advantage of the opportunities it offered. It would be wrong if I gave the impression that I was preparing for blindness; not so, but I never dismissed the idea that one-day it could be a reality.

I was grateful for the small amount of light that was getting into the eye, it made me appreciate what most of us take for granted: our sight. With that attitude life took on a new twist as I became more self-confident, radiating a happy and cheerful outlook. As the eye healed and I observed more light the images became bolder and my stress levels sharply decreased.

Excited with the changes that were taking place, I decided to spring a surprise on Catherine and tell her. I could see her smiling face – she was pleased. What was significant, like my first experience of images, I was afraid to tell anyone in case it did not last. But the new discovery overwhelmed me so much that I could not care less whether it was long-term or not. Catherine was over the moon with excitement and the telephone became too hot to handle as we passed on the news. It never occurred to me that things could change for the worse by the following day. I believed the restoration process had begun and there was no turning back in my case! Amidst all those setbacks, the loss of my livelihood, my independence to get up and go whenever and wherever I wanted. Driving the car or travelling the countryside, pastimes I enjoyed over the years were no longer an option in my new lifestyle. I should have been feeling rather pathetic. Yet I was at my happiest. The disability had shown me the other side of my life, which was richer in value than the one I had been pursuing all those years.

While I set myself the task of helping others, the blind association had volunteers who had organized a fishing weekend and invited me to come. Well I hit the ceiling with excitement; absolutely fabulous, I thought, just what I need to take away the fears that were festering about the school. But how would I manage, I thought? I could not see the line or the hook, let alone cast out the rod? I was grateful for the opportunity, but terror was eating away on the inside. For a while I allowed myself to be dominated by negative thoughts, which were quickly discharged. Soon the organiser John was on hand assuring me that those thoughts were the least of my problem, if there was one. John said "There will be volunteers who would be our eyes throughout the match." Oh, that was music to my ears. My dumfounded appearance gave him cause to ask the question a second time, "Would you like to go fishing?" I almost fell off the chair with shock. I never thought the day would come. I thought my fishing days were over – gone with the wind. Casting a line and with hooks – am I dreaming?

Fishing is the only sport I was ever good at. In earlier years as a young engineer, my friends and I joined one the local fishing clubs to take part in several competitions. I made my own tackles, apart from the hooks. What made it easy, my engineering workshop carried the materials, such as wire and lead. These were the two ingredients I needed. Designed and built with an adjustable mould for the weights, which was vital to the game. On windy days, waves discharge obstacles along the shallows, making it easy for expensive tackle to get snared amongst the debris. Using weights helps enormously. The area we normally used was peppered with huge rock-boulders, acting as sea defences, but gaps between each rock created an added obstacle for the tackles. The lost tackles were greater in number than the fishes we caught. Making our own gave us an added scoop to develop and create new shapes and sizes, which were outside the standard sold in the shops. That did not mean ours were better than others, it was up to the fishes whose bait they went for. The new tackles also allowed us to have healthy competition amongst ourselves. Watching the would-be expert trying to match our distance of cast was fun. Their standard equipment would fail to produce that kind of performance. We would also have a smoother return with less snagging. Echoes of laughter would fill the place when we beat them at their game. They had no idea we had made our own tackles, which worked extremely well if the weather was right for those particular sizes.

Sadly, as life progressed we took on more responsibilities and became parents with demanding children who increased our workload, which took priority over fishing. That wonderful pastime was allowed to slide into obscurity, leaving most of the tackles broken, taken by the children as they tried out their skills on canal banks. Those custom-made pieces that gave us hours of pleasure were left amongst the weeds and rushes.

The opportunity to recapture those bygone years when the fishing line slipped from my fingers, the specially curved weights rocketed through the elements toward the sky leaving a trail of line flowing like a bird on the wing. It bowed like the rainbow and fell into the water, sinking to the bottom in the hope that a fish would devour a tasty muscle of bait.

Those magical moments as the competition heated up, the elation, the joy, the grins that engulfed the faces and gave us young ones a perfect platform for healthy reverie against friends. It also enabled them to understand that 'good enough' is not acceptable, but that we had to do better than our opponents.

As parents we love to extend our skills for the benefit of the children so that one-day they too will inherit the wisdom we injected into work and play. Those thoughts have taken me back to my twenties when I was young, fit and full of enthusiasm.

Old and cranky, my fingers have lost their touch, not to mention my eye, whose sight like my youth was just a wishful thought. I needed to know if a blind man could cast a fishing rod. "Yes, please count me in", I shouted. I still had a few bits and pieces of tackle plus my pride and joy, which is a rod and reel of high craftsmanship still in their carrying case. This gathering would be on Sunday, and it would extend over a five-week period. The event was to be held on series of man-made lakes that were situated in an idyllic part of the countryside, between a backdrop of mountains and a winding river.

Paired with a volunteer, my day's fishing begins. Soon my memory was flooding back and in a short time I got into the swing of things. A tense but exciting start made me call on my rusty brain to take in the coaching I was being given: how to hold the rod and the stance I should use. The feel of the gut between my fingers sent shivers down the back of my neck. A few trail casts and I was soon mastering the craft.

The day wore on and one by one fish were being caught by the other competitors. Anxiously I waited for my moment of glory to come, whilst the fishes stayed away from temptation. For a moment my thoughts began to play tricks on me and a period of doubt began to cloud my judgement. Did my guide put on the right bait? Was it enough? Why weren't the fishes biting? But, soon I was shouting like the rest in ecstasy, reveling in the glory of my catching my own fish. The elation was visible for every one to see or hear, yet I was fearful that the fish would slip from the hook as I reeled it in. At first I could not see the little beauty, even though it gave me enormous pleasure as it fought against being caught. At the water's edge, reality dawned and my excitement was too much to contain. My joyful noise summoned others to take notice of the catch. My guide secured its landing and put the fish out of its misery with a sharp blow to the head, extracted the hook and placed it into my hands. For a brief moment I felt as though I had wet myself, which was too embarrassing to mention. The spirit of competition began to riffle through my body. The urge to catch another and bigger was compelling. I could hardly wait to have the rod and bait, and recast for the big one. A fish at my feet! This recaptured the magical moment I longed for and made me want to scream. But what was more exciting was that within a short space of time another fish was fighting on the end of the line. I could not believe what was happening. To have caught one was great, but a second catch in a few minutes, it was more than I could do to control my emotions.

People at the lakeside thought I was barking mad, or I had a hook in my leg. Many of the other volunteers were running to my rescue, but they came for the wrong reason. It was a beautiful trout flipping on the end of my hook! The fish created ripples among the group, while my head became swollen. The caps I wear became difficult to fit, I was so proud. I could not believe it was happening and that I was part of it.

They were a good bunch of people; they congratulated me and cheered me on to more catches with a less exciting outburst. I was given a stern warning that it would be their turn next. So if I had any notion of catching another before them, I would be used as bait. It was wonderful to recapture the feeling of youth. Commotion erupts as my exuberance exceeded the tranquillity in the valley, but it was my moment of exltation. Two of the fellows escaped the anguish of my exuberance because they were unfortunately totally deaf. Moments of sheer madness like these were good for the soul, just what I needed to release my tensions.

The perfect day of fishing ended with my tally of two fish each weighing approximately three pounds. I proudly took them home and in excitement I extended a graphic description of those exhilarating moments to Catherine. She loved fish dishes, but preparing one for a meal wasn't part of her scene. I did the deed, wrapped and placed them in the freezer. By nightfall the excitement petered away and I was ready for the following day. It had been the tonic I needed.

# Chapter 8

## THE NEED TO LEARN

The volunteer friends working in the community continued to invite me to their meetings. They constantly badgered my brain to lend them my experience in helping to further their project, which brought me into the realm of writing. Having to attend various meetings and listening to complaints arising from the community, it became increasingly difficult for me to communicate properly when presenting a case of an individual's concern to the group. That meant the use of words and sentences that the readers and listeners could understand clearly. Disorientation from the tragedy left me in a terrible dilemma. Unable to read small print, had my brain had shut down, leaving my vocabulary in tatters?

Memories were an act of bravery, which was a struggle for me. The volunteer organisation was pursuing an interesting kind of work for the community and if achieved the residents would embrace the benefits. As a boy I went to school and did well, I studied Engineering and reached a position of responsibility. So I was aware that clear, correct communication was vital to my survival. During those years I have implemented various successful working practices, which earned me a great deal of respect. I thought the volunteer assignment would be easy in comparison to previous experiences. But the conditions weren't the same. I could not see to read, which was an important part of the work. Handing out information that wasn't clear to an unconvinced participant was a recipe for disaster.

What they were developing was a basic adult education and computer course, a combined project. That was a great idea and I thought it might be the answer to my problems. I could go back to school and get my brain into gear. I arrived home that day feeling pleased with myself. Catherine was busy carrying out her house duties. Filled with excitement I interrupted her flow with the news that I was going back to school. The shock caused her to drop the article in her hands, she said, "What school, are you going bonkers? And what about your eye. Do you want to loose the little you have? What brought this on? Oh, I know it's that group you have joined." She continued, "Aren't you afraid of causing more damage?"

A few minutes of exchanges while I convinced her that this is what I wanted and that I was prepared to suffer the consequences, should they arise. With trepidation she acceded to my demand, providing I was willing to give in at the first sign of stress. Feeling on top of the world the following day, without a guide, I went to see Benji. During the conversation I casually allowed my intentions to flow through. Again from a concerned friend I was given the third degree before he relented and wished me luck.

His support was of great importance. Their vote of confidence consolidated my strength, which drove my dreams of becoming a student. Looking ahead, one day I would read clearly and concise communication would be possible. I was preparing to start at the bottom. I needed help and I was ashamed of that decision. Working my way from the bottom would dampen my enthusiasm and restrict the speed at which I was proceeding. But, it was the nearest venue available to me and that made me capable of dealing with my situation. Brain stimulation was the key if I was going to be a successful member of the group.

It was 6.30 p.m. on a Monday evening; my friend and I took a walk to the High School where the new project was being set up. Housed in one of the buildings, it had easy access, which suited my disability. We looked around, making sure that it was suitable for adults and not kids' stuff before making the final decision. It was also important that my efforts did not become a big joke. A scrupulous inspection was necessary. Sharing a classroom with youngsters who flouted the rules of law and refused to attend school would tarnish my street credibility and jeopardise the respect I received. Although I wanted those guys to follow my lead and endorse the program, I was nervous. Its casual approach aimed to lure the disobliging back into learning.

Peter – a Scotsman and a friend who had reached retirement age – was fit and young looking. He carried himself well and commanded a lot of respect within the neighborhood. An auto-mechanical engineer with the aid of computers, he wasn't keen to engage in the type of learning program I advocated. The new project was just what I needed to kick-start my dormant think-tank, so I took advantage of it.

Arriving at the classroom, I was welcomed by a teacher who was in charge of the staff for the project. We introduced ourselves. I did not know at first that she thought I was accompanying my friend. What a laugh! She led us to her table, one of several which had four chairs creating a square pattern and she explained what the course was all about. Looking around the huge hall I saw dividing screens separating the classes. My class was for basic learning and beyond was a bank of computers, twenty or more. Because of my blurred vision I was unable to see any youngsters in attendance. Sitting, the teacher insisted on being addressed by her first name 'Kay'. This attitude of informality removed the pressure of being in a classroom. I told her of my circumstances and my difficulties coping with my condition, yet I have this overwhelming capacity to learn. The precise words I used, "I need to have my brain stimulated, so I have come to regain some of what I have lost." "You have come to the right place," she replied. "I will do my best." She was over the moon hearing those words. Well the smiles got bigger as her face glowed with excitement. Her welcoming attitude encouraged my optimism which hasn't faltered to this day.

The layout of the hall was intimidating for a nervous person like me. There was a bank of computers seating twenty students merrily pounding away at the keyboards while on the opposite side, tables and chairs were waiting for the teachers and poor old me, who was starting at the very beginning. What was wrong with that? Entering the hall I found myself in a desert of space creating the seclusion a student needs. Peter wandered off to the computer section in which his interest was greatest, even though he did not find the concept stimulating enough to warrant his immediate acceptance. His reaction was "I've seen it all, done it

all, got the tee shirt" which was to me, folly. During the interview
the teacher probed my ability to cope and drew up a plan of
action and carefully established working times. Twenty minutes
per session would avoid excess strain on the eye, which would
have put an end to my new start.

That first week tested the determination of a man who
encouraged and advised those dissolute kids to return to the
classrooms. I sat in a classroom with some of the same youngsters who were progressing merrily in their computer studies,
while I learned to read and write all over again. It took a lot of
courage, yet I wasn't really aware that I was so courageous. To
accept my condition without feeling a right prat is very rewarding. Well, sometimes I did believe some of the youngsters might
think I was a fraud, especially the rebellious ones. They would
have had the right to think I could not read. Yes, such thoughts
have crossed my mind and I wanted to hang onto hang onto the
macho personality that was so precious to me. My fears led me
to understand how the children felt, having to grow up more
quickly than nature intended. With a boring childhood, going to
school did not seem helpful in solving their identity problems.
After all, there were times when I got silly feelings by having to sit
in a Basic English class, which was exactly how they must have
felt amongst their friends. Like me they wanted to be macho.

My growing capacity to learn put me into a nervous frenzy. I
lacked confidence and was afraid of failure. How ridiculous it
would have looked to those younger fellows, if they were to
become aware that I could not carry out a simple educational
function. It would cause disillusionment among the very people
I was striving to help. I was also fearful of being condemned
before anyone knew the facts about my affliction. A unique
opportunity presented itself to experience some of the intimidating pressure those youngsters experienced as they tried to
compete with their brighter and more fortunate friends. This made
me more determined to get my brain back into gear, and to turn
decline into positive action, producing the kind of project the
community desperately needed, one I would be proud to present
to the group.

One might tire from my long-winded monologue, but it is important to understand how degrading it felt at 55 years of age, sitting alongside a sixteen-year-old, who in the course of my work would give a penny for the guy. With those and other kinds of gestures I was looked upon with respect as an intelligent man, who had solved a number of their learning problems. It is hard to explain an invisible illness, such as the loss of vision, which depresses the sufferer but is disguised by an almost normal behavioral pattern so that others cannot realize the extent of the handicap.

Kay, the tutor, realized from the beginning that I wasn't a dodo and that there was something worth saving. As the number of lessons mounted her brain-teasing techniques began to stimulate my whole being. The thoughts it created allowed the work to flow, my lesson time increased, my aversive pose faded and confidence took root. The simple unassuming Lady, yes I said "Lady", presented herself as an aide to the class regular teacher who, she was the English teacher who never said "No, I am busy – wait!" She allowed free speech. There were no extras, no frills, no hidden agenda, but sincerity, yes they was her qualities and such qualities rarely surface in the modern world. She had years of experience working with people who have learning disabilities with impaired vision. What made her more than qualified to tackle my situation? Matching her qualifications to her personal qualities gave her the right ingredients to encourage my desire to learn. Her simple approach and encouraging gestures made learning easy. She knew which button to push, and how to push it at any given time. Kay was quick to acknowledge that I have grammatical impediments (broken English), being born outside the United Kingdom, but she pointed out that it wasn't a problem if used correctly and in the right contexts. That comment immediately hit the settle-down button. She said, "People live in the north and south of the country, taught by the same teacher, yet they speak with different dialects." So I had nothing to fear. She was there to make sure I used words in the right order. To demonstrate how bad I was, I try to create these lines:

They said I was too frail,
My eyes were in a daze.
A venture from my maze,
To an open cage.

In school I learn words
At church I praised the world.
Grow up to my dismay,
To find it was the wrong day.

A casual walk to the class
Greeted with a smile.
Heart thumping in thought,
Am I doing right?

She said I was good
Destined for the top,
I thought I was stuck
Till I write a book.

I take what seems a joke
To Kay's learning crave,
She prods and pokes,
And starts a writing craze.

Within a few weeks my brain gets into gear, an appreciable change
was taking place. What had been a fleeting glance, suddenly
switched on the stimulating process that woke my sleepy brain
to life. The boldness generated by colleagues and me went into
the community, and by example, encouraged those people the
program aimed to help. A massive invitation drive motivated those
people who were too shy to take that first step. I had led the
way.

The beauty of the summer's day warmed my presence and
helped with confidence building. I was constantly interrupted as
people sought reassurance that there was nothing wrong about
going back to school, regardless of age.

Part of Kay's and my strategy was to write a few paragraphs in the community newsletter with the headline, "Roy comes out," which caught on and did exactly what was intended. One could interpret whatever they wanted from those lines, but it has done the trick, making people sit up and read the article. They soon realised there was no embarrassment in learning. After all how many of us can remember what we have learnt at three years of age? Not many I think.

As I write the story my vision has improved. Accepting my capability taught me how to take advantage of my disability correctly, which is what counts. As the eye grew stronger, Kay introduced another of her ace cards, which was the best thus far. It came in the form of an invitation to the Education Centre, where she worked full-time, to look at a specially adopted computer program available to the visually-impaired. She assured me that I had nothing to lose by going to observe it.

Monday came and off I went to the education centre, and she reminded me to "go and have fun, enjoy the change and remember, you're not on your own." Those words 'fun,' 'not alone,' gave me the final push to take on what seemed an impossible task.

I arrived at the centre to be greeted by a bunch of happy faces, staff and students alike. I was also told about a special teacher, who is extremely good at training students like myself at using the computer. That was comforting to know, because she explained the computer was fitted with a special program to make the lettering as large as I wanted. It got better by the minute. I continued talking about the computer and this special teacher, but I could not help but wonder whether she was getting fed-up teaching me, seeing I was the only one she taught at the community school. After all, we were just beginning to appreciate each other and that school environment. Being there was essential to my role in the community project. It was to encourage residents to take advantage of the facilities that were designed to improve their educational standards. Although I was enjoying the benefits of gaining the skill to use words more effectively, that venture was an enormous mile-stone. I faced the challenge of new teachers and students, learning computer skills that had been alien to me. There was only one other person who like myself had impaired vision – a total stranger. I heard about her, she seemed a very understanding person, but the pressure was still immense.

I should have been there at eleven-thirty in the morning for my introduction to the class. Instead I arrived at twelve thirty pm, an hour later. I was asked the reason why I was late? But I could not give an answer. Instead I frowned at the thought of making a fool of myself in front of the students, which was silly, I know. The decision Kay has taken was in my best interests, but it left me with cause to wonder. After all she had been teaching me for one year, which was time enough for us to develop an understanding. When we first met we explored each other's background, and she revealed that she too had come from the Midlands a place where multi-racialism dominates a large section of the population. My first address was in the Midlands. Her experience in teaching people with substandard English is how we forged a connection. It gave us a basis for trust and identity, which grew with confidence and with time.

Filled with apprehension I saw people's faces light up like the morning sun. It was a repeat of my first encounter, as if someone had switched on a record player. My teacher was full of charm as she said, "Hi folks, this is Roy, and he has come to join us!" I was terrified but somehow my quivering lips separated to expose those beautiful white teeth, which everyone mistook for a smile, while the corridor outside echoed with sounds of laughter.

The room wasn't tiny, but with the amount of students and equipment that it housed one wondered whether it was safe for a person with my disability. As I entered the room, on my left was the coat-hanger which held a number of students' coats, while on the opposite side were wide windows which allowed maximum sunlight to penetrate the room, which in turn radiated warmth and happiness to us its occupants. The computers, the accessories and the chairs neatly laid out along the adjacent walls gave the place life, while in the middle of the room, a number of tables the same height were pulled together to form one enormous one, which seated approximately ten people. At first glance I was horrified, thinking that getting around the room would be a nightmare. To say the least, I wasn't happy one little bit. I was going to bump into those chairs from time to time and someone might think I was drunk or being silly.

Till then I had been dismissing the truth of my disability, so suddenly admitting to all and sundry, was difficult in my case. So yes, I felt threatened someone other than my family was about to know more about me than I want them to. But I needn't have worried. Their smiles and their welcome assured me that they accepted me completely.

Kay introduced me to each individual student, who, with wide grins and sparkling eyes, cemented my position among them, giving me a seal of approval. Those actions set alight the flame that has gone on burning brightly inside. She introduced me to the computer buff "Jim" to whom she pointed out aspects of my disability. It was also noted that Jim would be my teacher and mentor. Whatever I wanted to know he knew it and was willing to share his knowledge. He was a big fellow, six feet tall and about fourteen stone. Jim had one of the most infectious laughs I have heard in a classroom. It was absolute magic when he let rip a few echoes from his repertoire. The whole class vibrated with relief from any tension that might have been lurking. His charm and composure eased its way onto my case as if he known me for a long time. It was comforting to know that there are people like Jim and his sidekick who came in the form of 'William' a real trooper, dedicated to the art of computing. Within an hour of my stepping through the door, Jim and William dismantled my thoughts into pieces. They then took the pieces that were infected with doubt and cleaned them with alternatives, lubricated them with fun, and reassembled them with laughter.

Their action was a direct result of Kay's request to teach me the skills I needed to help stimulate my brain and sparkle my zest for learning. With an open mind I accepted the challenge. However thundering through my head was a great deal of hesitation, worrying about the limitation of my capability. Will I do well? Am I making a fool of myself? The bottom line was that I could not afford to let my community down.

As the class progressed it became clear that I had to surpass my own expectations, what seemed to be my goal for accomplishment continuously changed and I was excelling beyond my wildest dreams. Three hours with those students passed faster than I ever knew that time could. I have spent many hours in classrooms throughout my life and I have yet to find a comparison. The time ticked away so rapidly that I was surprised to hear Jim say, "Okay everyone, see you on Wednesday." I was given a short interview with the man whom I have come to love and respect enormously, along with his assistant William.

During our encouraging talk he pointed out the opportunities and facilities available, specially adapted to suit my condition. His advice was genuine, which took me back to my first encounter with Kay. To put those events into words and on paper gives me the opportunity to relive those great moments. But as I record those events an overwhelming feeling of gratitude captures my thoughts and prevents me from using simple words of description. This meant using my trusted friend, the dictionary, which created problems for my eyes because of its small print. Still my brain yearned to find the words to illuminate my thoughts, in order to satisfy my hunger to learn. I was forced to stay within the bounds of words that I know and to say things simply and clearly. That's what I want to achieve.

At that stage my determination to learn was in tune with my enthusiasm. Thanks to Jim and William's encouragement, any hesitation and fears slowly cantered through the window and escaped with all the carbon monoxide that floated merrily in the atmosphere. Jim a big man in both size and voice was well-versed in knowledge and culture and he used words exquisitely. When he spoke the words flowed as gentle as the wool from a lamb's back. His voice gave me the feeling of delicate smoothness, something tender to touch. His smiles radiated round the room and sent the dust from the books floating through the atmosphere like plumes of smoke from a steam engine. In that strong but gentle baritone voice, he called his assistant William over to join us. Oh my goodness, talk about Laurel and Hardy; Jim and William were doubles in size and in their manner of approach, even in the way they would start and complete sentences. Bless my soul! I was about to be taken over by a replicant pair.

William was always smiling, one of that rare breed who smiled when their eyes are open, and not from any joke or funnies. He would greet me with a smile, leaving nothing else to do but return the compliment. The irony of it all, neither man deluded anyone with their smiles because they were genuine. Jim told William about my special circumstances and instructed him about what program was suitable for my needs. William was the ideal person for me; already he had someone close to him in a similar situation, so he was capable of dealing with my disability with sensitivity. For me, they were the ideal combination, a story to unfold to bring happiness into my life.

The interview came to an end and Jim unleashed a small rendition of his jokes to captivate my thoughts and send the dust scrambling through the window like a flock of wild birds. Two steps through the door and I congratulated myself for having done the dreaded deed. The day had gone better than I had anticipated despite the wobbling knees.

Buzzing with the excitement of that wonderful day I made my way down the two flights of stairs which were fitted with a beautiful grey non-slip covering. On the wall were pictures of drawings and notices about the school activities hung in descending order, attracting my attention. On the opposite side was the slow-moving chair-lift attached to the stair rails? Earlier that day I had been too nervous to notice the interesting surroundings. The entrance and the reception area were at the foot of the stairs and as I continued my exit, the sunlight burst through the huge window at the top of the stairwell lighting up the place and showing off its charm, as if to say "This is where beauty prevails." Leading to the roadway were five flights of steep-angled steps with no markings. After a successful and relaxing day I totally forgot those awkward steps. Head held high with smiles from ear to ear, I calmly made my way until I reached the last tread of steps. Stepping down to what I thought was the street level I went head over heels onto the road, allowing my bottom a chance to kiss the pavement. In my hour of glory I just happened to walk on the deepest end, miscalculating the depth, and down I went like a sack of potatoes.

The enthusiasm and wonder-boy syndrome was knocked from my system – I wanted to yell for help. The street was busy with people but I doubted anyone would care. Still, two women came to my rescue. They asked 'if I was okay and if I needed help,' and I replied by saying "I'm okay thank you." I rose to my feet, brushing myself down and feeling rather foolish as I nursed a bruised pride. What must those women be thinking of me? A drunk perhaps, or a drug addict, and I am neither. One minute I was a vibrant optimistic fellow, walking tall as I stepped from the classroom, next I was reduced to disillusionment and fear. I had a fright, but I remembered the ladies who helped me even though the street was busy with people.

The shock reminded me that I was where people could see me and so I tried to regain my composure and act as if it never happened. With dignity I continued my journey, fighting to erase those thoughts of negativity that ground my brain to pulp. I certainly did not want to have another fall. I decided to complain on my next visit, from then on they decided to make the edges of the steps more visible to us partially-sighted people. A white line was painted on the edge of each step. That would break the uniform grey colour that dominated the area. With a sore bum and bruised pride I continued towards the bus stop, clutching an extra subject in my repertoire for Catherine's ear.

# Chapter 9

## MY CONFESSION

Casually I made my way home with an appetite to give Catherine a right old ear bashing. But when I arrived on the doorstep, the cat was mewing away, which I thought unusual for her. She sometimes waited at the door and cried for Catherine, but not for me, even though we had become good friends. Her ears shook and a feeling of foreboding began to overcome. That triggered off the wondering game. Could it be Danny?

Although I have come to respect the man, he wasn't my favourite person, not on that bruising day. I stepped through my front door as though I was a visitor, not knowing what to expect, whereupon Catherine interrupted my entrance to warn me of an unexpected visitor, who was a cousin called Albert. I was glad to see him, but at the same time also furious with him. After all it had been more than two years since I had been struck down with this setback and it wasn't as if he was living in a foreign country which he couldn't leave. Nor was it as if his wife and children were too ill to be left alone. The postal and telephone services were not out of order. So what excuses could he have from not getting in touch with me? Moreover that evening I wanted to share with Catherine the excitement that was bubbling inside. I was desperate to convince her that the new brain-teasing exercises would not create a problem for my sight if they were done within the training safety guidelines. Instead I had to explain the missing years of my life to that big-headed twit who was only interested in himself. I was not looking forward to this as I had a miserable existence as a child in his company. Before I could say hello and ask how he got here, I had already decided that he wasn't wanted, because I had a crippling confession to make, and the time wasn't right to unload this burden. I never thought I would say this, but blindness does have its advantages. During his visit, when he said something that wasn't conducive to my ear, I found it not be too difficult to answer in strong but respectful words. Why? Because I could not see the expression on his face or his body language, I spoke to Albert with strength and conviction, with no respect for his facial expressions or his body posture. I sat grimly in the chair and listened to him offering consolations and sympathy and making promises I knew he could not keep. But as the saying goes, a promise is a comfort to a fool, which I think he was unwittingly trying to endorse. Soon Albert was given a cup of tea, while my trusted friend Sofia the cat sought comfort in rubbing her head on my legs. A surge of revengeful thoughts went through my head. If only I could get Albert to feel the same I would have felt much better.

Albert was four years older than I was and during our childhood, growing up together, he always took great pleasure in making me do the things he didn't want to do and was very domineering. In other words, I was his fetcher and carrier. My value was demeaned which allowed my resentment to flourish and fester as I grew into adulthood. During those years I prayed for the day I would be an adult, which would give me the right to get revenge on him. When the time was right, it would be my greatest confession. One event stood out over all.

We both lived in the same house and each day we would scout the area in search of employment. One day Albert returned after an exhausting morning of job searching. In his search he collected a number of vacancies. He would get me to apply my skills in answering the questions because I was good at that sort of thing. I was the brainy one, so it was up to me what I wrote on the forms; total trust was given to me. He gave me the freedom to do whatever I wanted. No one doubted my ability. Answering the questions for him, I saw myself as a mug, once again doing his work for him, which would make him even more domineering. Worst of all, I could still hear the sounds of his bad attitude buzzing in my head. The temptation for revenge became stronger by the minute.

Well I was ready and willing to process his forms, more so than at any other time, yes I was about to inflict my educated weapon onto his job prospects. He was so sure of himself and my obedient nature that he had no idea that I was up to no good. I took the application forms to my room where it was private, since after all there was no need for him to be present, and I already knew the answers to all the questions. Armed with pen and envelope I commenced the evil deed and decided to spice it up by adding a bit of comedy to the application forms.

Name:      Jack Misfit
Address:   21 Isle of Dogs
What job would you like? Jumping over the moon.

I mailed them with no return address. Every day that followed, Albert would look out for the postman hoping for a reply. I did not know at the time that one of the application forms was a mere formality. He had already been given the position and only had to present the form before starting the job.

None of the jobs materialised. I wasn't exactly proud of myself, but I feel much better, knowing I could make him feel as bad as I had been feeling over the years. Until this day Albert hadn't a clue why those jobs fell through and I dared not utter a word about it. An act which I bitterly regretted, but we were young then and I had no experience of tolerance. Relaxed he sat in the chair and spoke of his present position and my face gleamed with excitement at the memory of those days. If he knew the truth then I wouldn't be writing this story.

With some remorse I apologised in a roundabout way, by saying I was sorry for not staying in touch, although my real apology was for my misdemeanour. His visit helped me unload the guilt I had been carrying for many years. In return, Albert renounced his bad behavior during our growing-up days and in a way I took that to mean, he was repenting for the wrongs he done me. Even now, though, he stopped short of those magic words, "I am sorry."

After hearing him saying how silly we had been and he being the eldest took advantage of his age gap, bullying us the smaller children I was relieved, knowing I could put to rest something that had long been a thorn in my conscience. It was also clear that he was more conciliatory than I feared. He offered to stay and be my eyes and transport to the various places for a few weeks, the hospital, doctors, school or an outing. He was willing to carry out the role of minder. But I could not take the chance having him around in case I had a slip of tongue and spilt the beans. With dramatic posture I pleasantly declined his generous offer. I think he was relieved and so was I.

That feeling reminded me of a similar shock I endured at the age of ten. It was also Albert who created it then. We were all at the river, where the waterfall had gouged a deep hole. The place was teeming with children, some diving into the deep end while others like myself played on the banks. Unfortunately some of us smaller ones could not swim at the time. But it did not stop us playing at the water, provided we did not exceed a depth above our knees. This safety margin wasn't good enough for Albert. All us non-swimmers were wimps according to him and should be taught how to swim, so with his big-boy attitude, he over-powered me and threw me into the deep end! Bobbing up and down trying to scream, my arms flapped like a doctor bird feeding on nectar, swallowing mouthfuls of water until someone came to my rescue. That afternoon visit made the whole episode more meaningful. He has messed up my day. I'd been looking forward to the pleasantries I was hoping to share with Catherine. So, what would life be like with him around for three weeks, bedlam, I think? Yes, I was glad when he finally said good-bye and went.

Albert went home and left me with a bruised pride and a battered conscience with no interest in recapturing the enthusiasm I had during the journey from school. Instead I was left with the task of telling Catherine about Albert and his position in the family tree, because she had not had the privilege of meeting him. The evening wore on; Catherine grew more tired of the visit and her day's duties did not leave her in a good frame of mind. Further waffle about my ambitions was of no interest to her. So we sat in silence while our minds gathered strength from our calm and relaxing bodies.

Soon it was bedtime and nothing more said, although, I'd reawakened my desire to speak with Catherine. But, although I was boiling away on the inside with all I had to tell her, my chance had gone. I should have been able to unwind but instead I became more hyped-up than at the beginning of the day.

I was feeling fed-up with that evening's events because I had not gotten my own way. I decided the only solution was my bed and to leave it all for the following day. I rose from my chair, ploughed my way through the passage and up the stairs. Now all I could see at ground level was gray in colour and looked like an unbroken surface, even a lump would give the impression as being level.

# Magic

Sofia the cat had eaten something that had upset her stomach; and in her wisdom she thought it would be a good idea to return the meal on the stairs. Halfway up the stairs, my feet lifted high and hitting the stairs with a thud. But, then suddenly instead of a thud – it was slush. "Oh my God," I cried. "What is this I have stepped into?" It felt like a puddle of ice-cold jelly covering my foot. Unable to see what it was I became hysterical to say the least. In shock my heart felt as if it had left my body and fallen into a bottomless pit. My initial reaction was to touch my feet and feel what it was, but I was too scared. Once again I screamed for Catherine. She wasn't long reaching me. "Stand still!" She commanded. I started sniffing at it, hoping to detect a smell I could recognize. Luckily my nose could not get close enough and the smell did not compare with any other around the house.

By this time Sofia was nowhere to be seen. However she had been at the top of the stairs sleeping until she heard the sound of my voice, which sent her scurrying for somewhere to hide. I am sure Sofia knew she had done something wrong. Why else would she exit the house at such an alarming speed? Mind you, I was so frightened, I did not hear, or feel the wind from her body as she whizzed past my feet.

Catherine gently held my foot and removed the offending matter that was causing distress. Although my feet had been cleaned of all the impurities I still had the feeling that it was there. A bath was the answer. A good wash, which did not excite me one little bit. What should have taken a few minutes, getting up the stairs, undressing, and having a quick wash then into bed, seemed endless. Sofia's action caused a few hours of depressive emotions and a near-heart attack. Nothing could have prepared me for that sort of eventuality. Any thought of getting hold of Sofia had to be abandoned, she was nowhere to be found. Catherine tried her hardest to call and reassure her, but she had decided to stay out of our way until the following day.

With my adrenaline as high as a kite, I got into bed hoping that sleep would come sooner than later. To my surprise, I did sleep. I opened my eyes, the lids partly sealed, and after a few seconds of gentle persuasion they opened to a room blazing with sunlight, while a cuckoo bird perched on the window ledge and sang praises to the dawn of another beautiful day. The experience of the disastrous evening disappeared from my mind; instead I went looking for Sofia who by then should have been at my bedside mewing to be let out. Her absence reminded me of the night's escapade, but I was worried about her so I scrambled down the stairs in the hope of finding my friend. Up until then I had no idea of her whereabouts, she seemed to have slept outside.

At the back door a ball of gray fluff was waiting to come into the warmth and safety of the house, apparently oblivious to the disruption she had caused. She was mewing for dear life, as if to say 'What took you so long.' "Good morning," I said, her paw tapped me on the leg reminding me it was feeding time. Her plaintive cry rekindled our friendship and soon she was devouring a hearty breakfast, while I joined in with a cup of tea.

Having drunk my tea I was still eager to tell someone about the excitement of yesterday and my hope for the future. I was like a child waiting to ride his or her bicycle, too excited to stay still while other children were already having fun. I was itching to ring my friend Benji and to tell him in chapter and verse what was happening. The atmosphere was electric, my brain was frying but it was too early in the morning. This gave me a few minutes to reflect on what Catherine and Benji had said in the past.

They had been concerned that I wasn't giving the eye time to heal. My desire to write could strain my already weak eye and could cause long-term damage. Of course they had a point. Doubts began to surface and I thought long and hard whether to continue my craze, but I was stuck with the same conclusion. There was no guarantee my eyesight would get any better even if I gave it maximum rest. Working my eye at a reasonable pace was giving it exercise and in my opinion healthy living would help it to become stronger.

Those peaceful hours of reflection helped to seal what I had already decided. That was the genesis of this book. Each day my determination grew stronger and my brain absorbed more information as I tapped into a writing talent that I never knew I had. By the time Catherine was awake the urgency to tell her my decision for the future had passed. In its place was a feeling of calm, as if I had already told the important people, and so there was no rush. I think the most important person I had to tell was myself – and I had already done that.

To understand why my eye should suddenly hemorrhage when everything in my life was going smoothly was very difficult. It appeared destined that I should discover a new path in life that had never occurred to me. One thing I am quite sure of, whatever twists and turn life takes, I was willing to accept them as they unfolded before me.

I must confess that during the first few months of writing, I have suffered severe pain, and I could not identify whether it was caused by overwork or a reaction from the medication. But, I was convinced that the next day would be better and that optimism made the days pass quickly.

So I had decided if I was going to be blind, so be it. But as long as I could see to put pen to paper I would write. My Christian faith steadily become stronger and led me to believe that there is a greater power at work where my health is concerned. Looking at the daily events and the sequence in which they occurred, no matter how perfectly the script was written, as long as humans were responsible for its execution something was bound to go wrong somewhere. In my case, there were setbacks, but no disasters; nothing went so radically wrong that I wanted to give in. Accepting my limitation gave me courage to excel beyond even the greatest expectations.

## Determination

Schoolwork and attendance began to fill my daily routine. Confidence played a key role in my volunteering work and my social life progressed with lots of fun thrown in for good measure. As the saying goes "A laugh a day keeps the doctor away."

Jim the gentle inspiration encouraged the dreams for excellence in his students and they did excel. With such encouragement we could not let him down. Kay on the other hand continuously encouraged me to write a story, something about my life. This would help me, she said, to get accustomed to the computer in a more leisurely fashion.

I was very nervous of the machine and it made me feel like a child in my old school facing my former teacher Mrs. Wolf, a lady who spoke with her strap at the ready. She had been short but very flexible with her strap. If we gave Mrs. Wolf a wrong answer then there was no escape from that strap. When her class moved up to the next, we had memorized every word, whatever subject she taught.

At the computer and scared out of my wits, I was always tapping the wrong key causing chaos to the program. William spent hours working out programs suitable for my disability. His approach was patience. In all his introductions he stressed most vigorously that to be patient is to give oneself time to understand the subject and it will become easier with time. I listened and observed his simple but effective methods which helped me to develop my capacity for learning.

Soon I was to fulfil my dream, writing a project report putting into operation what I set out to achieve for the volunteer group. This was to be my first test of my educational exercise. Jim's casual and fun-like presence reduced the tension, allowing Kay, my teacher, to guide my efforts in a way that made my brain work hardest, using unfamiliar words to express myself and to add new meaning to my life.

The assigned life story was also progressing rapidly. Four pages had been written. My vision stabilized and probably improved but that wasn't noticeable yet. I had memorized and adapted to the layout of my surroundings so to the onlooker my sight appeared to be improving. The relaxing atmosphere in the class-room helped me to be composed and to control my ego. Those pages made good reading, which gave me the idea to write the story as a Christmas present for my children. Every year I had given cash, or bought material things that didn't give an enduring message. Giving them the written words about their heritage would be a momentous thing. It would last throughout their lives and teach them their history and their roots.

That idea rang many alarm bells in Kay's ears, and those of Jim and William. They thought it was a brilliant approach. To hear those people endorse my idea opened a floodgate of thoughts, which set my motivation-motor into overdrive, and gave real impetus to my writing.

I put my eyes on those massive letters the screen projected and my fingers on the keyboard, I rested on a specially built platform which compensated for the erratic vision that occurred. I hoped my children would sit up and take note of the story. For one thing, it would be a surprised for them to know that I have enough limited vision to be able to write. The family would be enlightened to know about the journey from my native country, Jamaica, and how I managed during the voyage. My imagination ran wild with the thoughts and ideas that were piling up. I could see the expressions on their faces. My eagerness to write meant that I was unstoppable, but I was still unable to put words together that made them readable. I was no longer thinking about the disability that plagued me, nor did I worry about what would happen if the eye got worse before my story was finished. All that was defeatist talk and I would not be part of that.

Every day I sat to write a few pages, only to find I would read it all over again because Kay would put her red pen across some of the words, which changed my meaning and lost some of the emotional impact. But Kay pointed out that I had to make it communicate with the children. Kay's approach worked. She helped me to reconstruct my words to convey the meaning I wanted. It was frustrating work because I couldn't always find the words I wanted. But Kay could always give my mind and soul a voice through the words she would help me to use. I wondered whether Kay knew how fed up I would get and how often I wanted to pack it all in. Kay saw something in me that I did not know existed. I was good at telling the story orally, but putting it on paper in a readable format in a way that would give the readers excitement and interest baffled me.

Her diversion worked a treat, and I enjoyed the collaboration with her because it stimulated my imagination and made me more determined. As the weeks passed the number of corrections mounted in tandem with the increased number of written pages. I also got an extra buzz from the way in which Kay read the material. This was evident after she carried out some corrections. She would get hold of a paragraph that was well put-together and read it out to the whole class which gave me a tremendously satisfying feeling. Those moments of elation always landed me in trouble over my diet. Being a diabetic I had to maintain a balanced diet, with a steady intake of food and drink. I would frequently disobey this rule, leaving my body short of the nutrition it needed and that would result in a drop in blood-sugar level, which would make me hypoglycaemic, feeling weak and helpless.

Jim's deep baritone voice would ring out, making sure everyone worked to the correct safety guidelines. He would shout, "All those who have been sitting around the computer for more than an hour, stop now go and have a break." There were times when I cheated, there were moments when the work became over-powering and I couldn't leave it. So I ended up as a black man telling a white lie. I knew it was the wrong thing to do, but my interest in the story became obsessive. To make matters worse I was writing more new material and adding to the list of corrections that I already had to do.

My motivators Jim and his sidekick William were there to put things right and set me going again. They took notice of the urgency I placed on learning as my work increased. There were moments when my eagerness got the better of me and I punched the wrong keys. Sometimes I would do terrible things to the program and I would have to delete a lot of work.

## William

William was a good computer technician and taught me the language brilliantly. One day he came up with a fantastic suggestion and offered to sell me his computer. He suggested it would a good idea to consider the possibility of buying my own computer. He said, "The amount of work you are doing and the speed at which it is being done warrants your own." Listening to his words, I was flabbergasted. I could not believe my luck and for a minute I was speechless. Someone woke me up from this dream and suddenly the words came out "Yes please, thank you!"

My reaction came amid laughter as if I had been told a rib-tickling joke. He looked at me with a shocking expression, as if to say 'Are you going mad? Have I said something to upset you?' The idea of owning my own computer was both exciting and terrifying. I regularly messed up on the class computer so where would I get an expert to sort me out at home? I needn't have worried. William decided to sell me his old computer knowing it would last a few years. Better yet he was prepared to teach me how to use it, which was absolutely brilliant.

His offer was gratefully accepted and I bought the computer. He installed all the software leaving me to do the things I dreamed of. I was let loose to do whatever I liked, but my obsession developed into a monster. It wiped out my will to keep to my diet and it turned me into an uncontrollable beast who ignored my body's demand to stop work. I knew that only practice would give me the skills that were needed. So when I switched on the computer, my focus was on how fast I could learn even if I had to work all through the nights. Achieving what I set out to do was more important than anything else. This unreasonable activity was ridiculous to everyone but myself. My obsession almost cost me dearly. Continuing at that breakneck speed, losing my sight would probably have become inevitable before my book was finished.

Accessing information from books such as the dictionary I found that the print was too small. That impossible task hindered my learning process. The keyboard was another thing I had to master, so I concentrated on the co-ordination between my eye and fingers, and that concentration bothered me a lot and caused pain in my eye. The pain in my eye was probably due to that and to the medication I was taking as well.

During the days that followed I kept telling myself that the next day would be better and time whizzed by. But fears of blindness kept nagging at me. There was no getting away from it, so I decided to keep working as long as I had enough sight to do so.

Having taken that stand I experienced an amazing surge of my Christian faith in everything I did. My will to win became stronger, to the point that I felt sure that there was a greater power at work and all I had to do was to carry on to the end.

Looking at the daily events and the sequence in which they occurred, no matter how perfectly the script was written, as long as humans were responsible for its execution something was sure to go wrong. But not in my case! There were setbacks but nothing went radically wrong, to give me cause to feel dejected. The acceptance of my limitations gave me the courage to excel beyond my own expectations from which I got a continuous buzz.

The changes and excitement that occurred in my daily routine made it more obvious that to care about my body and diet was of great importance. I spared no effort in charting a healthy course hoping that it would allow me to stay healthy. I didn't want to have any kind of breakdown. But my sight did not deteriorate, instead it steadily improved.

I pushed my new freedom to its limit. I would venture into the town without an escort, trying to rebuild the confidence that I'd lost. During my independent walkabout I found that sighted people showed a lack of interest in the visually impaired. They crisscrossed in front of me and constantly knocked me. Some pedestrians failed to notice the cane in my hand. They were too busy scurrying to reach their destinations. But that wasn't always the case. Someone would misjudge his or her steps and bump into me. I was disillusioned by such behaviour. I wished I could do something about that selfish behaviour. I became aware of the difficulties the sighted have noticing the disabilities of others. But if every individual were to give a little more space, the problem would become minor. The trips into town became more and more frequent and my spirits rose with each achievement. As I continued to conquer my fears, the joy I felt forced me to share the experiences with Catherine, making her listen to me. She reacted with calm amusement to my quest of changing the world. I thought about the past and compared the days of my humble beginnings, with the present. A disabled person used to be given help in coping with their lot. But, now in spite of the political and cultural changes that supposedly help disabled people the two things that would help most – respect and courtesy – were missing.

It was also an enormous struggle for a migrant person to introduce changes in a society where hostility prevails against minorities and education was slow to divert illusions. I find myself thrown into a culture alien to me. The tolerance and respect my parents taught me during my early years had served me well, but I have found it to be a rare commodity in today's culture.

# Chapter 10

# READING

My writing improved daily, and I was also working on the corrections. Christmas was drawing near and so was my deadline for finishing my task. Luckily my work was on track. My work for the community volunteer group was scaled down, so I could give undivided attention to writing my story. I had to apologise to my volunteer colleagues for not doing the things I had promised, but I had to write my story. I didn't want to give up and go out and buy presents. And because the teachers were in on the surprise, I had to persist with it.

Reading the written word was always a problem because it was impossible to focus on the print. Doing so made the letters look joined together. Another set-back occurred because I was not able to write for long periods and created pages of work without a break. I struggled to find a solution and eventually came up with a drastic plan of action. Swallowing my pride, I asked for help wherever it was available. Fortunately I did not have far to look, it came from my friend Lynne and my wife Catherine. Although I felt humiliated, they were very kind about it, and agreed to read the work which solved the problem. But what must they have thought of me?

I could not rely too heavily on the teachers; they had limited time with each student, making it difficult for either of them to read and correct my work. The family's help gave me an extra import to produce better-quality work for the teacher's appraisal. It also allowed them to keep abreast with the improvement in my health and the latest of my discoveries. The downside was to have mistakes pointed out by a family member which were sometimes like a like kick in the teeth. But, I had no choice because the completion of the story was my top priority and any help was most welcome.

Creative thoughts were pounding my brain cells, but there were difficulties finding the right words to give a clear and precise understanding of the notions I was trying to express. Writing a story set thirty-seven years ago meant that I had to dig deep into my memories and to relieve each event. And, if that wasn't difficult enough, I was at the time recovering from a period of disorientation, a by-product of that disaster which I suffered.

Somewhere among all that, there was a force giving me strength to maintain the continuity of my story. But, sharp on my heels was my next radical appointment. I was forced to stop all writing for fear that the specialist might find something wrong, which would have most certainly put a halt to my dreams.

Knowing the consequences of being foolhardy, I still wasn't prepared to wipe the slate clean. My behavior was no better than that of Danny, 'Mr. Know-it-all.' Why, the convenience of Catherine and Lynne's readiness to read, as I corrected the written work was too hard to resist. They enjoyed the reading, because it was news of the family history that was being told from the perspective of one of its members. I suppose they thought that one day those words might lead to a published book and perhaps I would become famous and they thought it would be nice having a celebrity among them.

During that busy period, a flaw in our relationship began to show up. Catherine was spending more time away from me and I was too obsessed with my work to notice the change. It wasn't that my love for her changed, quite the opposite. Her affections had changed. It was desperate for me to regain my literacy, so I was prepared to work even harder to achieve it. I must agree we weren't spending much quality time together. What time we did have was short and sometimes counter-productive. I often wondered why Catherine maintained the reading sessions, was it out of duty or curiosity? On the days she read for me, my heart beat with excitement. As I listened I sometimes wondered if it wasn't someone else who had written those words. Happiness refreshed me like rain drops on a hot summer's day.

Even though Christmas was fast approaching with lots to be seen to, Catherine needed all the help she could get from me; but she allowed me to concentrate on writing the story. Whatever else was going in her head, she did see its importance to the family. Once again she was left to take on the entire job of decision-making around the house.

Grateful as I might have been for her generosity, I could not help the obsessive feelings that dictated my every move. So much so, I wasn't able to understand why she helped me. I took for granted that every one would do what she'd done, regardless.

Those selfish thought left me with a baggage of guilt which took some time to disperse. I could only take comfort from the fact that although it was the last day at college, it wasn't yet Christmas Eve. That meant I had a few days left to get the packaging done.

The speed at which Christmas hurtled towards us seemed to exhilarate me while my typing speed stayed the same: slow. This forced me to work late into the night to make up for lost time. Surprisingly, the more I burned the midnight oil the quicker my fingers became even though I stopped frequently to ease the pressure on my eye.

The pile of pages grew as a novel took shape and my dreams became reality. By the time the Christmas break-up was only three days away, there was a pile of corrections to be done. Panic began to brew, my fuse ignited easily inflamed by nervousness and impatience. There were verbs I wanted to use but I had no nouns to go with them.

Everything had to done at school where the right equipment was available to finish the job. No-one really understood how desperate I felt inside. For the first time Danny's help was in demand even though I detested his overbearing attitude. At that particular moment he was forgiven. The count-down of days began to take its toll; but William came to the rescue. Once again sunlight lit up the dark corners and my heart developed a musical beat. My well-formed teeth began to show a sea of whiteness as the grin got wider. By the end of the day all the typing and corrections were done. My elation was shared by William, Jim, and Kay, who had done the final proofreading and given it her seal of approval. Hurrahs echoed from my lips and my soul rejoiced at the birth of my story. I was so pleased that my wishes have been achieved, the classroom took on a different meaning. The splendor of a mid-December's day with sun shining on the autumn leaves sent fruity smells drifting through the open window and encouraged the wandering bees in search of nectar. Inside the sunlight fell on our faces, all alight with happiness.

I was grateful yet nervous, as a fearful thought crept through my mind. What if the children didn't appreciate that kind of gift? How embarrassing to say the least! It was not a normal gift. What if my English wasn't good enough? Three months of hard work had come to an end; my emotions slowly subsided and peace of mind gently returned. I had one more job to complete: the purchasing of Christmas cards to cover the book.

Arriving home that evening I was filled with the Christmas spirit and the joys of accomplishment, behaving like a kid with a new toy. Catherine was preparing our evening meal. I uttered a hasty hello, but the sound was muttered, as though my tongue was in a hurry to pronounce a different word. My selfish attitude prevented her from answering the greeting promptly. I waited in silence for a few seconds and then my tongue, a deadly weapon, lashed with vigour till the sound of my voice echoed around the walls. I have finished writing the story. I was anxious to tell her the good news in a conciliatory frame of mind, but having no response to my jumbled hello, I was disappointed. Desperate to pour my joy into someone's ear I turned to the cat who was mewing at me and said, "Sorry, I am having no luck today." However if I'd had an audience, the telephone would have definitely been the thing to spread the news rapidly, especially through Benji and Lynne.

They had been instrumental during the construction of the story, so the big news should have been interesting for them. I wanted to shout out as loudly as I possibly could. Against all the odds a blind man has written a story. However there was a problem: I could not do it justice. It was impossible to read it with the fluency I needed and the story needed my voice to allow the listener to grasp the enormity of what was being said.

I invited Catherine to share my moment of joy, but she was

reluctant to precipitate in it. The tone I used was different from what I had been using on previous days. What had I done to attract that kind of reaction? Rebuffed, I began to think. Overcome with shame and disgust I was forced to apologize in a roundabout way, before retiring to bed. To seal my sincerity an extraordinary Christmas gift would be ideal.

## Final check

The date of my next hospital appointment for a check-up was getting close. However the heavy workload that had been placed on the eye wasn't giving me room for optimism. The thought did occur. A favorable result from the examination would boost my confidence and convince my carers that my eye wasn't being overworked. To give myself a reasonable chance I should have a break the preceding week to reduce pressure on the eye and allow it to rest. But I ignored that opportunity which was foolish. After all what is more important, my sight or mere Christmas presents?

With hindsight I should have given my eye the rest it needed. Deep inside was this unyielding feeling that one day I was going to be blind, so I thought, there was no time to waste in getting the job of finishing the story book over. Speed was my partner while I put pressure upon myself to work harder rather than to rest. Those were the thoughts I fought against when I left hospital. Now they came back to haunt me.

I was in a bubble of fear. Now, I would not recommend to anyone, the way I had gone about getting things done. Because I am not sure how I still managed to have my sight, however limited. The only ace card I held was the fact that I took care of my body by healthy eating. Whether that was the contributing factor, I am not sure. Time would tell.

I made the usual arrangements for the hospital visit – traveling by coach to the city and then taking a taxicab. On my arrival I was nervous, withdrawn and filled with apprehension knowing that I wasn't a model patient. My greatest fear was if the specialist found an abnormality. Though there was no sign of anything going wrong. Luckily I did not have to wait long, my name was called and the examination began in earnest. My nerves went to threads, worrying that the machine readings would be different from the results that I wanted. I began to entertain all sorts of silly ideas. It seemed to have taken longer than usual, even though my physical fitness wasn't in question.

Deep in thought my spirit drifted into "ifs": if only I had, if it were too late, until the specialist said "Jolly good, it's looking good." That was music to my ears. He went on to say, "Although the eye is progressing there is still a long way to go before I can assess the damage properly and see what else I can do." Relief came with a great big grin as I peered into darkness. Thank you. God, I whispered in a soft gentle voice. In gratitude I shook his hand and said "Thank you." Another appointment was made for six months' time, giving me enough time to get my story ready for Christmas. My memory is unclear whether he did respond to the handshake gesture. Catherine was pleased with the result and escorted me from his office.

All my thoughts were on my writing, so the journey home was a sombre affair. I had no interest in the surroundings or the things that usually cropped up while travelling. I became engrossed in the gift of sight. My brain searched for new words that would make the story more enjoyable. They were flooding my brain and I would find just what I wanted, which was good, but the trouble was remembering them. I never could. I arrived home loaded with those brilliant and dramatic words that I desperately needed, but by time I had got to the door I had forgotten them.

## Sofia

Sitting in the chair I poured out my anxiety to Sofia in the hope there would be a miraculous response, like a voice from the blue saying, "Shut it", instead she mewed as if to say, "I agreed with every word," but that wasn't enough to relieve the tension inside me. She wasn't interested in my writing, but rather the pleasure

the doubts and fears others had about me. This helped me to recognise there was something inside me that was worth pursuing.

Although my children had no knowledge of the written content, its intended destination, their congratulations were loud because of the fact I was writing a story. I could not blame their hesitation. I was in the middle of working through an illness, and to them I was just a disabled person. But my heart was bubbling to bursting point, yearning to give them a hint of what I had done. After all it was for their benefit, but I could not afford to let slip anything that would give the game away. This silence tempted me to get drunk to cushion the impact. That would have not solved the problem because I would have been in a state of drunkenness for two days which was the amount of time till Christmas day and all I had left.

Having to keep quiet for two weeks was a tremendous boost to my eye. Catherine and Benji were very pleased with the new silence that shrouded our home. Their eardrums rejoiced because my lips were sealed. They had time to listen to the birds singing or the children playing. I was forced to talk about anything but the story. Within the first few days of restriction, I came to realise how irritating I must have been, constantly bombarding them with the story and telling them of the experiences I had while I wrote it down. Now there is time to reflect, I can remember that either one would try to tell me to shut up, or to change the subject, but I would be so engrossed I didn't hear. Still I got more laughs out of Catherine during those two weeks than in the three previous months, which made me twice as happy.

## Reflection

With plenty of unrestricted time to do whatever I wanted. I began to examine my illness and the treatments I was receiving and what improvements if any. I was always testing my sight to reassure myself that the extra strain I had put on the eye had not destroyed the specialist's work. And, if there were improvement, my conscience would be relieved of any guilt. Surprisingly the result wasn't exactly what I wanted. The boost I was looking forward to did not materialise although there was no sign of deterioration that would cause alarm bells to ring. My vision was still in a mist and co-ordination between eye, hands and feet were not great, as I expected. After all, I have had three undisciplined months.

I decided to relax my mind and body and to allow nature to do what it does best. Once again the days began to pass slowly while I tried to find something to do within my capability; but everyone knew what was best for me, except me. Catherine, Benji, the volunteer group, and Danny all encouraged me to eat, drink, sleep and give the eye as much rest as possible. Did I take their advice? Yes, I had to. They made it hard for me to do otherwise.

Those days of relaxing mind and body brought on a surge of improvement. Changes had taken place in response to rest. With so much time to sit in my favorite chair and listen to stimulating music, I would drift off into beautiful and restful sleep. Those mid-day naps would prevent my going early to bed. I would not be tired enough to enjoy any kind of sleep. To overcome the restlessness I would pull the chair up close to the television to allow me to find a program I could watch. Flicking through the channels I was able to see the programs as they flashed on the screen. At first, I took it for granted that getting close to the television would give me better viewing. Suddenly switching from one station to the other began to take longer, because I was seeing and reading what was there – clearly. Still the penny did not drop. I would sit there for some time, unaware of the great phenomenon that had taken place.

Sofia came into the room crying as if to say she wanted to get out, and knowing her as I do, I got up with a struggle, to let her out. On my way back to the chair while listening to the dialogue coming from the television, half-way between the chair and the doorway, it suddenly dawned on me that I was walking in the dark. I was used to feeling my way around so light wasn't of great importance. Stopping at the doorway to get my bearings and focusing on the television light, I discovered I was seeing more than I had realised. The pictures were as clear as if I was sitting close. I was shocked, bemused, puzzled, and hesitant to move. Fearful of the changes my joints became weak from nervousness. Questions popped up in my head about why I could not see during the night, and not in the daytime. For a while they haunted me, but there were no answers. I was scared to move in case I was going off my head and was seeing something that wasn't there. In those first few minutes nothing made sense; my legs were too weak and I was afraid of falling over. I stood at the doorway for a few minutes before plucking up the courage to get to the chair.

# Chapter 11

## FEELING IT WAS A FLUKE

That night for the first time in one year and five months I watched a program on the television as if nothing had gone wrong with my eye. Feeling it was a fluke, thinking the television had put a spell on me, I began looking around the room testing the sight I was enjoying. I was able to see the wineglass, ornaments we had collected on various holidays, the pictures of my grandchildren, and to examine the beauty of my delightful stereo unit.

My heart and soul were in ecstasy as I enjoyed the experience of vision and hoped that it was going to last. Thank God for restoring my sight, but why in such an unusual way?

I was on my own late in the night or rather more like early morning, the cat had just gone out and Catherine was asleep. As far as I was concerned this was a miracle, putting my Christian faith beyond all doubt. Feeling so good that I did not want to watch the television any longer, I lay back in the chair, and closed my eyes and offered a private word of thanks to God for the restoration of vision. I drifted off to sleep.

I woke to the rising sun as the closing sounds of the television program echoed through the room. I had been sleeping for hours through that noise. I opened my eyes to the thought that I was going off my trolley. My vision was no clearer than it had been the previous day. So what was the early morning experience all about? Was I going mad? If someone was standing outside the door and had heard the conversation that had taken place, me with myself, it would be a clear case of something serious having gone wrong with me. I was desperate to talk to someone who would understand how badly I was affected by the changes.

Helpless, I sat hoping to hear a voice saying something that would have expelled my depression. The sunbeams through the window brought life to the household, while Sofia cried at the door to come in. Once again I rose, went to the door, and let her in, and at that moment I found it necessary to question God. Last night I was thanking him for the wonders of sight, but they hadn't lasted.

To save myself from doing something silly, I took the unconscious decision to wait until nightfall and re-test the experience. Catherine joined us downstairs in the kitchen, dishing up Sofia's breakfast. She casually asked "Why didn't you come up to bed?" Well at times like these you have to be economical with the truth so I said that I had fallen asleep and had just woken up.

Throughout that day I was a very worried man, I was in a hurry for nightfall to prove that I wasn't going senile. In order to keep it to myself I avoided contact with my friends in case we had a conversation that might lead to last night's episode. Even though I knew Sofia would not tell anyone, I could not take the chance that someone might overhear my conversation. It would have been disastrous to be branded a madman as well as a blind man. Luckily, I had no visitors and Catherine spent eighty percent of her time away from the house, which was a joy for me.

Evening came and still no change, my vision was still misty I had to feel for small or clear objects. To help my nerves relax I played some of my most prized music via the headphones. As my mind wandered I turned up the volume and sent my body vibrating.

I was in no mood to look at the television to check whether I could see what was on. At midnight I had discovered the elation that had stirred every fibre in my body, so it was only right to wait until then before I attempted any more disappointments. The music had run its course, my eardrums had become sour listening, but there were still a few hours to go. I went for a long bath. Having a bath would help to relax my body, and at the same time reduce the waiting time.

Once I got into the bath my body became so relaxed and time flew by. I emerged dried and dressed, ready to face any eventuality. I walked down the stairs and thank goodness Sofia wasn't there because tripping over her would bring Catherine to the sitting room. There it was, the television in all its glory beaming out a variety of beautiful colorful and flashy programs guaranteed to entertain its viewers and I was about to join them.

First glance and it was instant recognition. My distance was the same as the previous morning. I was seeing just as clearly, while my heart once again danced. At that moment I was ashamed for questioning God, because I did not have the knowledge to understand what was going on. The fact is I was glad to regain what most of us take for granted. Watching the entertainment was sheer joy, but after a few hours the eye became weak and painful, which led me to take some painkillers and wait for another night.

Retiring to bed I realised that a fundamental change had taken place in my brain, which I knew nothing about. All I could do was to make the best of what I had. With no writing obsession to occupy my brain, watching the television filled the void. But like writing, I was having more discomfort, as the strain of watching the television began to take effect on the eye. And, what was even more damaging, I was also crying out from depression and loneliness. Catherine seemed to have a limited amount of time to spend in my presence or with me. We were slowly drifting apart without any apparent good reason.

## Sets the diamonds alight

There were frustrating moments as I contemplated losing the business and all that I had worked for. I was learning to cope and accept the new situation and how to deal with it. Also the effect it had on my responsibility, as head of the home, as the provider. This did not help Catherine to be a happy and contented wife. I could identify how and when the slide began.

I invited her to join me in a visit to the town jewellers, where I purchased two very specially made gifts. They were very expensive items. I thought she had worked hard with me on the story, as well as the extra duties due to her mother's illness. I prayed the gifts would inject some light-heartiness and lift her spirit, so once again she would glow. After all we were entering the season of good will, Christmas time. What she did not know was that I had ordered those items weeks prior to being ready at that moment. Although she might think otherwise, it wasn't a sudden impulse.

Meticulous planning had gone into designing this pendent, its particular weight and size, which I knew would make her the envy among her friends. I checked the size as the goldsmith placed this magnificent piece of artwork around her neck. Her behaviour was exactly as we expected. Catherine's face lit up every corner of the shop and set the sparkling diamonds to shine like stars in the midnight sky. There was so much happiness, if the clocks could have sung they would have sounded like a thousand voices in an auditorium. My heart went into overdrive, my knees shook, my lip quivered, I was lost for words. The jeweler and his female assistant quickly gathered round to echo the excitement of approval of the elegant gift. Congratulating customers entered the store, making her the most special of them all. They must have thought I had just won a fortune, or was a rich person to afford that type of gift.

Catherine took the gift I was supposed to put under the Christmas tree, deciding that Christmas had come sooner then expected. She always wanted to wear it from then on. She was happy and so was I. Thank the good lord I have done something to make her feel extremely satisfied.

Feeling very special, Catherine's smile was as wide as the ocean and her eyes bright as the morning sun. I wish that moment could last forever. She seemed to accept the appreciation, love and gratitude that I put into that gift and I felt glad that all seemed to be well.

## Visit

Hilarious, Benji invited me to sample a refreshing jug of light refreshment, which was an excellent idea. An evening with him and other friends, all ready to have a good laugh at the drop of a pin was just what I needed.

He knew it was just what I wanted to restore my happy-go-lucky attitude I once possessed. Later that evening, I bathed and splashed lovely smelling after-shave over my body, pretending to be a glamour boy out to catch a gorgeous lady. What a laugh, looking at myself in the mirror, from what I saw, I was looking far worse than I had led myself to believe. I once sported a well-presented beard, which now had grown out of control. I had no desire to look smart and worse I was unable to recapture the memories of my sighted days. Furthermore the obsession to write was pressing so I hadn't been bothered about the overgrown hair. But the sight of this hairy-faced person in the mirror sent a shock wave though my brain. I asked myself questions like, did Catherine notice how dreadful the hair made my face look? But that kind of talk might tip the balance. She was still riding the cloud from the Christmas gift. I had aged twenty years and could not afford any more disruptions.

The evening sun brightened the sky, and there was a cool breeze, so the one-mile journey became a pleasant stroll. Our arrival at Benji reshaped my life, meeting old friends and indulged in a glass or two of beer. I was feeling concerned over my appearance, and so I quietly asked Benji if he would cut the hair on my face to make it look tidy. "Happy to be of service, he said. Will tomorrow be okay?"

I soaked up the attention and my heart overflowed with happiness, while my jaw became inflamed from the pain of laughter. I was feeling good and basking in the sunshine of health. It was a great evening. Struggling to get a grip with tired jaws, it become clear to me how much of my life had been wasted away. I had stopped doing the things that used to come naturally. To be in the company of those friends was a wonderful tonic. Between the fun and laughter I analysed the picture in the mirror, which led me to understand the meaning to lots of greetings: how well I was looking. I was being treated in reverse! I looked terrible!

Those people enjoyed my company, my smiling face presenting the image they had known and loved. Realizing the extent to which I had projected the wrong image, my heart sank in disgust while I questioned my pitiful behavior. And, at the same time I puzzled why someone within the family, or my circle of friends had not told me how badly I looked. If only I could have seen the reflection I could have changed my appearance.

A few days later I was summoned by my friend to carry out the transformation. The idea was to turn a rough looking face into a charming and delightful one.

The remaining days to Christmas gently ticked away allowing anticipation and many other mixed feelings to grow. I was concerned over whether the children would accept the unusual gift, and more importantly would they read it. I was interested in getting their reaction to what I had written, but suddenly I felt an unwillingness to deliver them. To accept those gifts out of politeness with no feedback would have hurt me deeply. Once again I found myself making a problem before it happened. Anxious to understand their feelings I reverted to my childhood days. Even though our parents did not have the same means to provide us with Christmas gifts we children would accept gratefully what we were given. After all they were grown-ups so we thought they knew best.

Children from any period love to have gifts they have asked for, or money. Money gives them the power to buy whatever they choose. They also get the opportunity to save, to build up a bank balance to use at will. Having cash as a gift, to touch, to count, to identify with its spending power brings an undeniable good feeling to a youngster. To be given a story written by uneducated blind man would not be quite the same. I was in turmoil wanting to know if I had done a good job and if they will like what I have written. Their reactions were vital to my future. The writing torch was burning furiously inside me. Having been smitten by this new craze did not mean that I knew what I was doing; far from it. The days when my brain was young and ready to adapt to learning new skills was long gone, and the disability had made it far worse. I had to be content with forces of opposition within my mind. One section would memorise the story, which was simple and straightforward, so I thought. The trouble was that my memories were not written down. Why? My disability made it difficult to understand the need for appropriate words in writing the memories down. While my mind struggled to put in order what was going on, frustration came into play, destroying good story-lines on many occasions. I survived those setbacks because I loved what I was trying to achieve. And furthermore there was nothing else I was capable of doing.

# Chapter 12

## STORY DELIVERY & CHRISTMAS

Christmas Eve came and my brain was relived from the unwarranted task of looking for nothing. As arranged my friend Benji accompanied me on the delivery of the unusual gifts. There were four children living within a seven-mile radius from my home, involving two bus journeys with four stops between them. Overcome with excitement of about this new form of achievement I proceeded against the odds of disappointment, and brought jokes and laughter to everyone I met as we went to make our deliveries.

The bus journey seemed short, which was not surprising given my mind's preoccupation with thoughts about the children's acceptance. It pulled up at the stop. Getting off the bus Benji began to say aloud what was troubling me. "What if they reject your gifts?" he said, "What if it isn't good enough?" I did not want to think about that possibility. We set out to find the number of the house, but on our way we noticed that the street was very quiet, as if everyone had gone into hiding from our presents. As we laughed and told jokes in the middle of a sunny day, a nervous resident looked on at a pair of strange men. At the front door we knocked and waited, hoping that someone was home, but no one answered the door. The curtains were drawn and it looked like no one was there. Disappointed there was no one to receive the gift and no one who would tell me how clever I was, I decided to post it through the letterbox. Great idea, but not without problems. The box wasn't wide enough to allow the parcel to pass without folding. Fuming inside, I searched for ways of leaving their gift without disturbing its well-wrapped and beautiful presentation. It was a dilemma; I could not leave it on the doorstep as roaming dogs might come along and use it as a tree trunk. Or at worse it could get stolen or wet (from the weather).

My disability made it impossible to return that day and the

following day was Christmas and too late as far as I was concerned. A solution had to be found there and then. As usual Benji would see the funny side and make a joke of it. Listening to his jokes, I found that he was in fact making a logical deduction about the event as it unfolded. He jokingly pointed out the length of time it took to write the story, and how I upset lots of friends and overworked my eye to produce a story I could be proud of. Now I had no choice but to bend the envelope and crease the elegant wrapping paper, and reduce its presentation to look like a rubbish bag. The neighbour's curtains were twitching and I imagined the occupants zooming in on my fumbling actions and the frustrated look on my face. In the midst of folding the parcel, Benji shouts "Let's get out of here before those twitching curtains call the police!" With that blast of decibels, I took his advice and quickly folded the parcel, and with a puff I poked it through the letterbox. To make sure, I listened as it fell to the floor inside the house. "Thank God," said Benji and we walked away, leaving the twitching curtains to resume their static position. Benji found the visit hilarious despite my disappointment. I can see the funny side now, but at the time that wasn't the case.

Making our way to the next port of call with the possibility of no-one beeing there to answer the door was too much to contemplate. With three other presents on my shoulder there was no time for negative thoughts. My youngest son and his family might not have been at home because they are busy people. It should not have been so surprising to find an empty house, but I was disappointed all the same, and felt as if everyone had done me wrong and I was wasting my time. That was a pitiful and selfish attitude which I did not admit to at the time. I realise that it was wrong to take such an attitude.

The next address was that of my third son. He had three children, two girls and one boy, who lived approximately one mile away. It was necessary to catch the bus if we were to finish the delivery before Christmas Day. His first daughter is the oldest and my first grandchild, and her reaction was of great significance to me. She was at that age when her individuality played an important role in the family. Getting to her house was rather awkward because of the steep incline we had to negotiate, but it was well rewarded by the spectacular view from their home.

We knocked at the door and bless my soul there was life. I was delighted. Benji was at his best with his jokes, so much so that those children were filled with laughter before I got the chance to greet them properly. After a brief hug and a lull in the laughs I presented the neatly wrapped story to my granddaughter in the absence of her parents. Their faces were aghast, they were looking for large parcels, or more than one small parcel. Instead they were given a book-sized parcel with some envelopes. Still they took it gracefully and placed it under the Christmas tree to await the grand opening. How I wished they would take a peek and tell me what they thought. Seeing they weren't willing to take the chance of looking, I had to break my silence. It was impossible to keep the suspense any longer, so I told them what was inside the parcel and hoped that they would like it. It was always a joy seeing those children and to share a laugh. It gave me a real buzz to see them that day.

Time was slipping away and darkness fell early. I was hopeless at seeing my way in the dark. The memory of those brief moments when I could see during the night to watch the television haunted me.

We had to hurry to the third house, where my first son lived with his wife and two daughters. What little beauties they were. This house was only half an hour away and mainly downhill, making the journey fairly easy. It did not take us long getting to their doorsteps. Arriving at the door was to be a surprise, but no sooner had I raised my hand to knock at the door it opened. They seemed pleased to see us, and greeted us with smiles hugs, and kisses, making a fuss of one another. Lots of pleasantries were being exchanged, but for now I wasn't urging any reaction from them.

Darkness seemed to be our enemy with its rapid descent. There was only one more house to visit – that of my eldest daughter, Andrea. She had been there for me through my illness along with my youngest grand-daughter, Angelique, whom I had christened, "my little beauty." Benji for the first time became subdued. He had total responsibility for my safety, because I was no longer capable of seeing where I was putting my feet. I took on the part of the joker, feeling happy that I had accomplished what I had set out to do three months previously.

To feel the hugs and kisses those children was heartwarming and to hear their laughter was music to my ear. In no time we reached Andrea's and Angelique's home and there was my little beauty, a ray of sunshine to brighten a dull day. Her sparkling eyes and white teeth greeted us with all the love I could have hoped for. She was quick off the mark to accept the presents and in a thunderous voice shouted so her mother could hear, she cried, "Thanks Grancha for the presents," which I know she could not read and so she would be unable to understand it for a while. I felt sure that her mother would read the story to her until she was old enough to read for herself.

When I gave her the envelope, which I pointed out was hers, letting her know there was a gift inside, her face dropped with a glimmer of sadness. Like most children she looked for the big parcel, because a big parcel represents the gift they want. All my doubts surfaced, a feeling of regret crept into my thoughts as the excited child turned into a bewildered one. Benji saw what was happening and in a flash he pulled out his master joke which sent us all into stitches of laughter.

My emotion got the better of me. I couldn't hold back the feelings of sorrow. I want to leave her company because the reality of that child's dismay made me question whether it was the wrong thing for a Christmas gift. I reassured her that we loved her and that although her gift looked small, I told her that its contents could buy lots of lovely toys. That word 'lots' gave her hope for a day out shopping with her mother.

Although I wanted the evening and my visit to last, it was impossible. The deepening darkness forced us to beat a retreat and head for home as fast as we could. Those deliveries left a bundle of mixed emotions. I wasn't quite sure what was the most important, the disappointment that no one gave me the feedback I desperately wanted, or the children's faces as they clearly showed that their expectations of large and individual presents was dashed.

One thing I am sure of, I came away a happy man knowing I had met and embraced those grandchildren I adored.

It was a tiring day. Benji made sure I got home safely, while Catherine was busy putting the final touches to the Christmas decorations, which looked good.

During the journey home, which was by bus, we had an exhilarating observation. We could not avoid noticing the sophisticated lights and decorations. The flashing sequences of lights created wonderful pictures of different animals and illuminated the houses and streets. The spectacle was worth watching, even though I had poor vision. I found the competitive spirit that thrived among the neighbours interesting. It was increased by the local paper which was to judge the best-decorated house in the community. Some of the exhibits deserve recognition for the effort put into them. Seeing them for the first time I was stunned by their beauty, the way their creators had used the colours of light to inject life-like animation into their subjects. Exciting stuff, I thought.

Benji was busy telling Catherine what sort of day I'd had. What she didn't realize was that he wasn't just explaining the day's events, he was cunningly winding me up. She burst out laughing when he explained our dilemma at the first address and the twitching curtains. It was easy in that relaxed atmosphere to see the funny side of the day's events. He said goodnight and left me in the comfort of my cosy armchair, with my music and my cat Sofia. Catherine was in the clouds and too busy to communicate. Wasting no time, Sofia was at my feet, and mewing as if to say she had missed me. I sank into my deep soft chair listening to music with my headphones on and wishing that Catherine would massage my aching muscles. Sofia was curled up at my feet. The pressure was no longer stifling me to achieve anything for the immediate future. There were no thoughts of writing another story, or of continuing the one I had just finished. I was just happy to relax.

Catherine was flitting in and out of the sitting-room, creating ripples of excitement. She was showing off her much-loved necklace and ring. More noticeably she could not do enough for me, which was disturbing at first; it had been a long time since she had been so attentive. Her actions made me nervous, wondering whether I had missed out or forgotten to do something she asked, or wanted doing. I counted everyone whom we bought presents for, making sure no one had been left out. She was wearing my gift with only the card left ready to be written and handed over the following morning. What could it be, I asked myself? Furthermore she did not want me to take any part in Christmas organising, so I couldn't think what might be wrong.

I desperately tried to reassure myself that everything had been done. It would have been easier to come straight out and ask her if I had missed something. But I was terrified of upsetting her, which would return her to those precarious days not long passed. I held my tongue firmly in my mouth and suppressed any urge to speak on that subject. Bedtime arrived to relieve me of that burden.

After a hectic day sleep wasn't long coming, which took me through to Christmas morning. I awoke to greet Catherine with a big smile and happy Christmas wishes. I heard the rustling and ripping of wrapping paper, and parcels being selected and put into order by my stepdaughter. This was the joy of Christmas, I thought.

The morning sun shone through the window and lit up the rooms, children's laughter invaded the house as they rode their bikes and skate-boards up and down the street. Sofia mewed as if she knew what was going on and wanted to be part of it. I made my way down the stairs to confront the usual shambles of parcels all over the room, but not before I went flying over one I did not see. Dangerous stuff, and my patience was tested, but I avoided that area. The rooms were beautifully decorated; the various coloured papers twisted and folded into patterns making the house a winter wonderland.

Leaving Catherine in bed, Sofia and I went out into the back yard, where I had one of the most disturbing moments I have had for a long time. As we stood in the middle of the pathway and listened, we heard a chorus of weird sounds. Every cat and dog in our cul-de-sac was making some kind of noise, and even Sofia joined in. It sounded like those animals were tied up in uncomfortable positions and were in pain. We heard the cries of new pets given to children given as Christmas presents. Their cries set off a chain reaction among other pets, but it was hard to believe that no one had taken advantage of those defenseless creatures. The mixture of sounds from the excited children and the howling pets made me wish that I was somewhere other than my home. Little did I know that this was to be my last Christmas at that address.

I sat and awaited Catherine's entrance, armed with her last remaining gift, hoping we would be together for many more Christmases. When she came through the door her smiling face conveyed happy wishes. I responded by getting up and hugging her, and wishing her all the very best. I gave her the card with more smiles and kisses. The rest of the day continued in that same marvellous spirit. We gave and received gifts, some we loved and others we could have done without. We visited friends for a quick drink and then disappeared, making the Christmas spirit worth preserving. Catherine continued to exhibit this form of total happiness as if she had been about to begin her dream holiday. The atmosphere was confusing for me. Somewhere along the line something wasn't as it appeared to be and I could not work out what. It took a further five months to reveal itself.

# Chapter 13

# THE BIG DECISION

Once the excitement of Christmas had been put to rest it was time to get back to reality. There were appointments to be sorted out with doctors, hospitals, and other places as well as arrangements to get to them. The most demanding of those was the school. I had to decide whether or not to return to the writing enthusiasm or to preserve the sight I had. A very difficult decision to make. The deciding factor was to be the results from the hospital appointment that was now only a few days away.

Everything worked out like a production-planning sheet: absolutely spot on. The specialist findings were favorable, even though I mentioned the new venture I was considering. What was pleasing was that it wasn't 'Mr. Cool' who carried out the examination but his colleague. He invited me to feel optimistic that my sight would get stronger. This meant that the writing could continue if I so wished. The journey from the hospital gave me time to think because the right decision was vital. I wanted to learn and to play an active role in the community, but my sight was more important than that. Next stop was the physician who would determine the state of my diabetes. If the results matched that from the hospital then I would go ahead, no holds barred.

As the days passed I created an invisible partner with whom I could relate all my fears and disappointments. What was interesting was that his role was to give the answers that I wanted to hear. It was a great partnership, and there was no one to blame if things went wrong and no one to repeat what was discussed. Any in-depth discussion on the subject with Catherine, Benji, or anyone else was vigorously restrained. Drastic as it was, my strategy worked and I made my decision.

Transforming my decision into reality depended on a good diabetes result, but that wasn't long to wait for. I repeated my promises to the community project, which had become urgent, and was putting pressure on me to gain the resources for it to succeed.

Three weeks into the new term and my school attendance became eratic. I was absent more than any other student. But I was determined to carry out my decision and so I cautiously visited the doctor to find out the results. I went to the surgery and surprisingly the place was virtually empty, the display screen was busy entertaining the empty chairs and magazines, and within fifteen minutes it began flashing my name. I was in and out of the doctor's room smiling from ear to ear as I had the result that was going to justify my decision.

Armed with the ultimate answer to three agonizing weeks of soul-searching questions, I continued with the writing craze. I hurried to the bus station, to catch the bus to the group's office where I could inform them of my intention. Grumbling travelers waited at the crowded bus stop dissatisfied with the service. I joined in and waited. Leaning on the side of the bus-shelter to ease my tired legs, the idea of writing the full story was intriguing. In some ways it was easy to understand why old sayings sometimes manifest themselves in positive ways. As one saying goes, 'what is to be will be.' Well, although the bus was crowded and late, when it arrived at the group's office instead of packing up to go home they stayed and listened to the news that they had been waiting to hear. I made a full commitment to the project. The joy and relief was plain, their faces lit up giving me a feeling of worth and value.

The aim for full commitment was simple. My intention was to introduce reports relevant to accessing the necessary funding. Knowing that I could not carry on with that kind of work without the help of the school exercises, I wanted to use the schoolwork to help me work on the project the community needed. That way I would gain in both ways. I would be able to continue with my writing even though the subject would change slightly and I would be able to continue with the volunteer role that I had committed myself to. I thought the right choice had been made.

What started with prospects and misgivings turned out to be a wonderful and fulfilling day, full of bright promises for the future. I walked through the door of my home filled with the strength of a lion and the memory of an elephant. Fingers crossed, my decision to take a low-key approach was at the forefront of my mind. But I had to be careful not to slip into any bad habits which could harm my sight. The very suggestion would bring Catherine out with all guns blazing.

I was fortunate to find that Catherine was with Grace, her mother, leaving me to tell Sofia my decision. By the time Catherine arrived home my enthusiasm had died and this left me free to talk about other events of the day without referring to my plans. Although I couldn't share my excitement with Catherine I looked forward to telling my teachers and friends the good news. Glowing with the prospect of finding a new beginning, I was falling over myself to get out and meet the people who had become the inspiration I needed. Benji in no uncertain terms warned me not to travel on my own, not even to the places I knew. My sight was simply not good enough to take on that responsibility. It was a warning I constantly brushed aside, in hope that nothing else would stop me from pursuing my goal.

A fire of eagerness raged inside me at that particular time. Every ounce of energy was focused on various eye-strengthening exercises that also improved my physical condition. To this day I am left puzzled about the urgency I placed on getting back into the classroom. I just wanted to continue my story and carry on writing, and of course to resume the friendship I had built up which had become too precious to abandon. Communication between my family and friends took a nose-dive as I was reluctant to share my plans with them.

That weekend was dismal, wet and cold, with a biting wind that seemed to get everywhere regardless of what I wore. I felt dismal too with no excitement in my heart. If the truth were to be known, I was a worried man. There was a baggage of uncertainty weighing me down. My mind was in a tug of war with the rest of my body, while my emotions behaved like an automatic door, opening and closing at will. The weather was awful with rain coming down heavily and getting into every part of my body.

I was feeling very sorry for myself as I removed my wet clothes and hung them on the coat stand at the classroom door. I felt lost and forgotten as if I were the only person in the world. My wet trousers stuck to my legs and I wished I were not there. However, the vibrating voices of greetings from my fellow students and teachers did manage to cheer me up, while from the far end of the room came a magical and poetical rendition of verses as everyone exploded in laughter and filled the place with excitement.

Jim had turned what was a demoralizing start to the day into one of insight and promise. We could have been forgiven for thinking it was a hot beautiful sunny day and the world was all right with itself. I took my seat at the massive table that dominated the centre of the room. Many of my student friends had individual tuition because their needs were greater. Kay and Jim had hoped I would return so my presence was of great significance. They had discussed my potential, based on the work I had already done, which left them with a strong belief that there was something in me worth bringing to the surface. Whether it would manifest itself, I didn't know, but I was back in the classroom determined to prove them right.

Kay kept on encouraging me to write. She wanted me to start again at the beginning, from my birthplace, my childhood, my emigration to Wales, and she instructed me to include as many interesting details as I could about all of it. In return Kay and Jim, with William the classroom assistant, promised all the support I needed, if the story turned out to be any good. She had really challenged me, and she had said, "The story you have written is interesting and warrants a more robust commitment," which was good to hear, although "robust commitment" sounded like a lot of hard work.

When I entered the school building, I dismissed any fears about the strain I might have put on my eye, but no sooner had I cast those fears aside than a new one came to fill its space, this time nothing to do with the eye. The excitement of the path on which I was about to embark began to highlight weaknesses in my ability to do what Kay had suggested. The success of the project meant I had to learn to use the computer more efficiently, especially to improve my typing. That was my greatest worry. Because in order to develop my typing skill effectively, I would have to spend more time at the keyboard, which is what I was hoping to avoid. However, even with that difficulty, writing my autobiography as I'd been asked to do was yet another stimulating prospect. My head spun and I thought of my mother, if only she had been there to share those moments! How fulfilling it would have been for her to see her son, the son she sent out into the world as a child, while she had to sit back agonizing. She would have been so thankful and so proud.

So how was I to begin? Where would I find the appropriate words to give clarity to the story? After all, I had just struggled through an embarrassing period. Unknown to me, the plans were already in place to reduce my workload. By prioritizing my requirements, I was able to improve the quality of my work. So my extra computing lessons were William's duty, while Kay and Jim both arranged the coursework to fit in with what I was writing. As the English tutor, Kay supervised all the reading and corrections and she knew exactly how to improve them. Having such programs prepared for my benefit was superb. I knew I had been right to return to school. With so much going on it had been hard to concentrate on just one thing. I still wondered what the family thought of their Christmas present – my story about coming to Wales. I'd heard nothing during or immediately after Christmas and the lack of comment was making me depressed. After working so hard to create such an unusual gift, having no response left me feeling that no one cared, or possibly that it had not been good enough. Yet amid all that negativity my teachers saw the story as a good piece of work that was worth developing. Their recommendation to continue the story was wonderful news and music to my ears. Although the children had failed to notice its potential, thank goodness the tutors had seen its historical value to future generations. I was given the ultimate challenge, and I knew how important it was, but without my family's encouragement, I felt not excited but numb.

Two and half hours passed listening to the new schedule Kay and Jim had prepared. Because emotions were running high I hadn't done much work. With so much to think about I was feeling a bit daunted. The story that had caused all this excitement was called, "My First Boat Trip," which told the story of young Roy whose parents sent him from Jamaica, his country of birth, to a foreign country, Wales, when he was only nineteen and a half years old. By law still a child, he undertook a journey of eleven days and nights aboard a large ocean liner which transported thousands of migrant passengers to the United Kingdom. Young Roy had to make decisions at his peril and to endure the nights on the ocean among strangers and adults: a nerve-racking experience for such a young man.

The story was put together for the benefit of my children and grandchildren as an unusual Christmas gift. It was an attempt to give them an insight into my beginnings, which would help them to understand their roots. Throughout my working life, remaining busy was easy. Accumulating money and possessions was good because they enabled me to provide for my family. But they cancelled out one of the most important aspects of life – keeping our family history alive, and I only now realised how vital it was to preserve it. The story tells of my introducing to the children their family history and also highlighted my tragic situation, and told what determination could achieve for someone who was willing to learn and fight for what they wanted.

The tutor's encouraging approach to the continuation of my story really made me want to do it. So I left the classroom at the end of that first grueling day feeling fully switched on and ready to talk about the things I have locked away in memory during my childhood years. With a shiver of trepidation lurking in my mind, I decided to be cautious and plan for one thing at a time, keeping my eye at the ready to record the past. It wasn't as easy as I had thought. Once again I was facing those horrible feelings that I might be resurrecting obsessive behaviors I had tried to get rid of. But I was so blinded by this unyielding appetite to write that it was easy to ignore anything that might create a barrier, especially worries about the fact that my health might be at risk. There was no time to dwell on trivial niceties since the story had to be written and I wanted to get on with it. A few days of soul-searching followed, about whether I should ask my mother to help. But I decided that putting the story together without her help would be a better surprise for her. Furthermore I wanted to tell it as I remembered, not the way others perceived it to be. Anyway it was being written for the benefit of my children, so it was important that they heard it the way I told it. I followed Jim and Kay's instructions, which was to write everything down that I could remember, even if some of the sentences were not in the correct order. They did mention that the written work would be read, corrected and put into chapters with some of the sentences cut and pasted into the right places, a process called editing. By the time I had got home that day, I felt I had aged considerably.

My story unfolded. I found it difficult to accept that the story was mine and that I was writing about my life. To make matters worse my English and grammar put me at the bottom of the league. While my brain dismissed the disabling setback I had been trying to overcome during the last eighteen months. I knew that I was using the story as a way to gloss over all that had happened.

Although I had already written a large chunk of it the opening paragraphs were causing me problems. I wanted it to be funny not dramatic. But I had no idea about how to arrange the words effectively. I was determined that no other voice was to be heard other than my own. I sat in the chair and closed my eyes, put my disability aside, and placed myself in the classroom facing Mrs. Wolf, the teacher who never used the strap sparingly. At the age of seven years in Jamaica I went to our community school and joined her class. Everyone of her students was neatly dressed in their school uniform, seams sharp as a razor. All were fearful of her, but I was terrified. During my time in her class she had an intimidating way of curling her strap which ensured that I listened carefully and tried to understand every word she said. Her voice rang through my ear, as if to say, "That's not the right way." That frightful thought steered my chosen words into a pattern that someone else could understand. I decided to start at the beginning: no frills, no fantasies, no dramatics, just the facts, covering the years from my second to my twenty-first birthday.

My computer skills continued to improve, which gave me the scope to produce more work while my eyesight stayed stable. The hospital and doctors' appointments became fewer and further apart, and the obsessive urge to do more became stronger. But I observed the strict discipline of the safety code which allowed my eye sufficient time to rest.

Looking back at the first section that I have written has given me the opportunity to take an objective view of that rigid behavior pattern that I have displayed. It could be looked on as a demonstration of strength, a way of proving to myself that my decisions were correct. I settled into a routine and time moved more quickly than I expected. The story developed into a novel-sized book, which was very pleasing, but the old problem of reading and correcting the work still dogged me.

Eight months soon passed and the book began to take shape. It was getting close to my mother's birthday, which was at the end of November. She lived in my brother's house across the Atlantic, in the United States. It stirred a lot of memories and created a desire to travel and pay her a surprise visit. That thought triggered off another brilliant idea: to finish the book as a birthday surprise gift for her.

Why do I always come up with these outrageous ideas I asked myself. They are time-consuming and damned near impossible. But a gift of that magnitude would really delight and re-assure her. Well it appeared that history had repeated itself. A year before I had done the same thing. I had many anxious moments but here I was preparing to do it again. As the possibility grew of having my Mother read the story I went to ask William if I could do it. He promised to help me and support me and I knew it could be done.

The book, like my short story, kept the same name "Journey of Choices" in the hope that it might make interesting reading among the Afro-Caribbean and other immigrants who came by ship across the Atlantic. The effects of having been sent on that voyage across the ocean with no sight for land of days on such a young person was both awe-inspiring and bewildering and many hundreds of thousands would surely identify with my experiences.

William devised strategies to allow the work to flow to its conclusion. He was a versatile person, having worked as a lithographic printer, with the knowledge required to organize the layout and the printing operation. What a stroke of luck; not only did I find a friend who could deal with my disability, but one who was also equipped to display my work.

William applied his skill of reading the lines of words to compile them into paragraphs, cutting my work into small chunks, and cutting out what wasn't needed. I was poorly equipped to deal with such drastic methods, and I grew Furious as I watched him doing it. I could not understand what was wrong. Such a good person, I thought. Realising there was an air of disquiet in my stance, quietly he said, "Be patient, it will soon be put in order." Within three weeks William rearranged the story; finished the graphics for the cover and completed the birthday dream for my mother. I will always be grateful for him and I was thrilled to think that I'd finished the story without any deterioration in my sight.

## Surprise Gift

The days shortened, and there wasn't enough time to get all the things I had to do. My departure date had been set, which seemed the right time to break the good news to my mother. I was right in anticipating her excied relief in knowing that my vision had improved enough to enable me to travel that distance. From the happiness that radiated through her voice, I knew nothing could have been more important to her.

The weather outside had seen much rain, wind, sleet and snow. There were flooded fields, overflowing rivers, rain washed streets, and drenched houses. The emergency services struggled to cope, and the hospitals were full to bursting point with patients suffering from the effects of the appalling weather. People yearned for warmth and comfort and for sunny places.

It was mid-November and the autumn weather was the worst it had ever been, giving an overwhelming urge for a holiday and the pleasure of spending time with the family I desperately wanted to see again. My visit was to their homes in New York, where from experience I knew that the weather is much colder, but not as wet. The lack of warm weather would be more than compensated for by the change of environment and the joy of meeting the family and friends. I itched with excitement.

On a Thursday I set out on my journey. Arriving at the airport my heart rate elevated from normal to supersonic as that organ fought to burst through the wall of my chest and explode. As I waited with nervous anticipation, my flight number flashed on the screen, which of course I could not read. However, a voice from the tannoy announced the call for passengers to make their way to the boarding gate.

There were many checks as immigrations were scrutinized by customs personnel making sure no one left the country without proper authorisation. I was assigned to an escort, and was taken to the plane and shown my seat while retaining my dignity. Happily, I made my way down to an aisle to claim the comfort of seat number 15.

A television screen was fitted to the back of each seat to give passengers an individual choice of programs from the on-board transmission. It took a few minutes to settle down as the big bird taxied. The plane sped along the runway and within seconds we were up and flying through the clouds like an eagle with its giant wings dominating the skyline. My heart leapt, now I was really on my way. Flying over the countryside forced my depression to slowly slip away with the passing wind and disappear with the seatbelt signs. A relaxed feeling came over me with the knowledge that I would soon be reunited with my mother and the family. In a new country, with new people, and different weather, there would be none of the stress I had been experiencing. I was looking forward to the close relationships that existed between my family.

There was a five-hours time difference. Landing later on the same day made the impact of the time change easier to take. We'd had a smooth and enjoyable flight and the stewards and stewardesses were wonderful. Their schedules were busy as they attended to our every call, making sure our comfort was their priority.

We touched down mid-evening; with plenty of time before bedtime to absorb the names of people whom I have not seen since they were babies. Another escort collected my baggage and took me through immigration and into the arrival corridor.

My first impression was that JFK was a huge and busy airport with a cold wind blowing unkindly through the halls. People were wrapped up like balls of wool, leaving me to wonder if there was a roof on the building. From the way they clad themselves I thought that New Yorkers' resistance to the cold weather was very low indeed. The whole place had a cold wintery feeling to it. Further, to my eyes the airport arrival corridor was poorly lit, with so many people waiting, most in dark colours, and this caused chaos to my sight. People were wrapped up, leaving only their eyes exposed, which made it difficult to recognise anyone at first glance.

At the end of a walkway, I was confronted by a young giant of a fellow. I could not see his face properly and his quick approach towards me sent shivers down my back. But when I could see his face properly I recognised him as my youngest brother whom I had not seen for more than fifteen years. Immediately following were another two brothers and my mother. I felt pure, unadulterated happiness as hugs and kisses came from all angles.

As soon as the initial greetings were over, we set off for my Mother's home, a journey of an hour and a half. As we drove, I became more and more impressed with the enormous numbers of elevated roads and rail that dominated the whole area making the place buzz with vitality.

The landscape was carpeted with high-rise buildings, offices, and apartment blocks. Travelling through suburbia, detached houses appeared, most with driveways, and front and back gardens. The average sizes were four stories with a basement where the heating system was situated. I was later to become aware that those houses were buildings to suit the size of the family. Either they needed a lot of space or the Americans liked to share the same roof with their extended families, hence the enormity of those homes.

Three brothers, two sisters, sisters-in-law, brothers-in-law, many nephews and nieces, and grandchildren gathered, with mother at the helm to welcome me. Words cannot tell the enormity of the reunion, knowing that I could speak freely, with the understanding that whatever was said stayed within the family, and no offence taken if a joke fell short of good taste. To relive childhood pranks was disturbing for some and pleasant for others. But they all meant the world to me.

We soon arrived at the gate of my family's house, which was to be my home for the next three months. The house was a three-storied building, with two basements, veranda, and large front gardens, a double garage and parking space for ten cars. With so many car owners living in the house the place looked like a shopping-centre car park!

I patiently waited for the right moment to present the book I had put together. Then came my proudest moment as I gave it to her – the story of foresight she had as a young mother, and what to me was most important, the journey I made as a young man to a strange country, and the decisions I have made which allowed me not only to survive but to prosper.

The room went quiet as she took hold of her present, and in shock she unwrapped the parcel, wondering why on earth I was giving her a gift in front of everyone, behaving as though someone had died. With the wrappings off, her eye zoomed on the pictures at the front and back, telling her that her son had written it for her.

The look on her face told the story as laughter, shock, tears, and amazement, all flashed across it, as everyone watched. Mother's reaction will always leave an indelible mark in my heart. Regrettably I wasn't prepared with a camera, so there is no picture to record the event. As she opened the book and turned the pages to read the handwritten dedication note she was overcome with emotion and retreated to her private room to be alone with her thoughts. The family were shocked to learn that I had lost my sight a mere eighteen months ago, that I wasn't using a white cane, and didn't need to be led around. Instead I had written this book, which was not what they expected.

New York is vast, there is no other way of describing the place, with skyscrapers dotting the land like dominoes in a Chinese game, and where everyone owns a car. Within a few days I began to understand the inhabitants and their way of life. I came to realise why they were always in a hurry, as if there was not going to be any tomorrow. First was the traffic, wherever I went at any time day or night, the only comparison would be the M25 Motorway in England. The other thing, a mile's walking distance, a few blocks away, if we went there by car, the journey would last three times longer, because of the one-way system creating queues of traffic. The other noticeable difference was when I stepped from the car and inhaled, it felt as if the air had come from a giant laundry. It was in direct opposition to what I had been used to in my town where the air smelt of tobacco fumes.

Being close to Christmas, the decorations and the sales drives were at fever pitch. Their behaviour was no different from ours as everyone fought for a bargain, while the businesses cashed in on the custom. My sister and I walked into this store, which was brandishing very large 'sales' signs with each section displaying notices saying items had been reduced from a to z in price. What was amazing was that someone had forgotten to cover up the existing card, which showed the original was the same as the sales price. We loved it, because we no longer had an appetite to shop and my sister and I left that store. It made me question the store's approach towards their customers as far as honesty was concerned. Apart from that, I must give them credit for their drive to sell at any cost.

The heart of New York City proved to be an extremely busy place. Yellow-coloured taxis dominated the streets, horns blowing as if it were life and death, while steam belched from the sidewalks, and people rushed like a panicked herd of cattle, and shoppers were badgered by merchants selling their wares.

There were bargains in the chaos. For instance, in one area, all the stores had wholesale prices, which was a very good idea. However it would not be my first wish to spend more than a day in that area. Other fascinating spectacles were the bridges, so huge I could almost hear what they are trying to say, such as, 'I am the greatest, come and try me,' and when we drove on them I saw the network of roads that rose to meet them.

The Christmas decorations were beyond all expectations. As the season approached, people spent a lot of time and energy transforming their homes and surroundings, creating beautiful scenes, encouraging visitors to travel from near and far to marvel at their wonders. The city rulers took pride in giving value for money, the way they lit up the streets and official buildings.

The family was a balm to my disturbed mind, their welcome and integration in particular. The joy of sharing life with them made me feel young, and brought back the memories of my childhood years. Sadly like all good things my holidays came to an end and I had to go home. I was leaving a triumphant welcome and congratulations for my exuberance from my family and friends. I felt as if I had just won the war for peace, and I thought of the support I had from everyone, especially Benji and Danny. They had unselfishly invested their time and energy to aid my recovery. But with all those good deeds nothing would have worked without my Christian beliefs and the obsessive, determined attitude to regain an independent lifestyle.

Four years later, my vision has improved marginally and I have adopted a new lifestyle as the hunger for independence grew. My computer skills surprisingly are developing beyond expectation and the obsession to write is still uncontrollable. No-one outside the family and close friends knows the extent of my vision, or of the fear that haunts me day and night – how long before I will be completely blind? As I forged through the no-quit barrier in writing this story, I have suffered extremely painful experiences both physically and mentally. Without repeating myself, putting the words on paper was the easy part, but reading the work, which is vital, is always a struggle. After all what purpose would it serve if the readers could not make sense of it? Benji, my friend, constantly reminds me of the pressures I have placed on myself, "Slow down," he says, which is a caring warning. But what legacy would I leave for my children, to use as source of strength to draw on in times of disappointments and despair? I have been a hard worker and I've achieved a few revolutionary things during those years. How long would the memories last in this rapidly changing world if they were not recorded? I ask myself. However, I wanted much more than that. I wanted my future descendants to know who and what I was. It was also important to reach out and encourage other unfortunate people who have suffered a disability of any kind to know that they too can search within themselves to find the hidden talent they might never otherwise have known existed.

The colourful display of inquisitiveness and laughter from my granddaughter Angelique ignites a flame of inspiration to look ahead and to take notice of what I had always taken for granted. Her appetite to learn, her willingness to help, gave me moments of sheer joy, even though I saw her as a mere shadow in a misty room.

I also recalled my faithful friend; Sofia the cat, she thought she was human but never quite made it. Her companion never wavered, as she played with me, listened to my moans and groans, with no talking back or giving the wrong advice or taking sides. If she were human she would be perfect. She will never be able to pass on this acclaim but perhaps cat owners will look at their pets with a more delightful feeling of comradeship. The story of my eye will go on to the end of my life. I might become blind before reaching the end of this story, but on the other hand the vision I have might remain to my life's end. But it is important that being disabled does not mean the end of one's usefulness to function effectively. Within us all there are hidden talents, if we are prepared to look.

My children and grandchildren will have a unique opportunity to understand first-hand what it was like when light turned to darkness. In my case, they will also know that darkness turned to light.